You Can Keep Your Parents At Home

Margo Arrowsmith

You Can Keep Your
Parents at Home

Keep Your Job and Life, Save Your Fortune and Sanity

Margo Arrowsmith, LCSW

Copyright © 2016 Margo Arrowsmith, LCSW.

All rights reserved. No part of this book may be reproduced, stored, or transmitted by any means whether auditory, graphic, mechanical, or electronic without written permission of both publisher and author, except in the case of brief excerpts used in critical articles and reviews. Unauthorized reproduction of any part of this work is illegal and is punishable by law.

Prior ISBNs
ISBN: 978-1-4834-1488-1 (sc) ISBN:

978-1-4834-1490-4 (hc) ISBN:

978-1-4834-1489-8 (e)

Current ISBN
ISBN: 978-1-944662-02-8(sc)

Because of the dynamic nature of the Internet, any web addresses or links contained in this book may have changed since publication and may no longer be valid. The views expressed in this work are solely those of the author and do not necessarily reflect the views of the publisher, and the publisher hereby disclaims any responsibility for them.

The information, ideas, and suggestions in this book are not intended as a substitute for professional advice from a physician and family counselor. Before following any suggestions contained in this book, you should consult your personal physician or family counselor. Neither the author nor the publisher shall be liable or responsible for any loss or damage allegedly arising as a consequence of your use
or application of any information or suggestions in this book.

Realization Press rev. date: 05/26/2016

To Fritz and Marjorie Arrowsmith, my parents, who gave me so much at the beginning of my life and at the end of theirs.

To Mrs. Betty Lange Houseman, my teacher, who recognized me as a writer when I was in the fifth grade.

To Rose Heffron, my father's best friend, who loved Dad and was the light of his last four years.

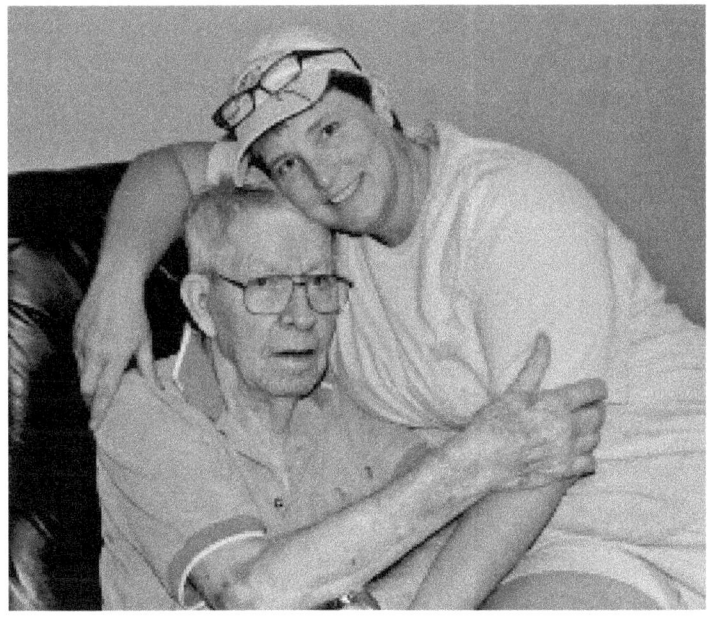

Rose was Dad's best friend in his 90's, a light in his life.

So the last will be first, and the first last.

— Matthew 20:16 (English Standard Version)

Dad helped me take my first step; I helped him take his last.

Contents

Preface xi

Chapter 1 How It All Started 1

Chapter 2 You Are Not Alone 5

Chapter 3 Know Where You Are Going 11

Chapter 4 The LOVE Formula 27

Chapter 5 How On Earth Did I Get Here? 31

Chapter 6 Let Go 35

Chapter 7 Organize 57

Chapter 8 Value 113

Chapter 9 Evaluate 129

Chapter 10 Moving Forward 147

Resources 151

Preface

My dad tried to take care of my mother all by himself. I tried to take care of my father all by myself. Both were mistakes. Fortunately, help fell into our hands.

I am very glad I took care of my parents; I wouldn't change that. But I wish I had been smarter. I am writing this book about my experiences—both professional and personal—to help you make the best decisions for you and your parents.

My mission is to help keep one million elderly parents at home, while helping one million adult children to be happy in their lives. I want to see a million good endings, like the ones I enjoyed.

My method is *LOVE*, an inclusive yet simple method that will teach you to *let go* of what is in your way, *organize* your team, *value* yourself and your parents, and easily *evaluate* where you are in order to make the road as smooth and rewarding as possible.

A test of a people is how it behaves toward the old. It is easy to love children. Even tyrants and dictators make a point of being fond of children. But the affection and care for the old, the incurable, the helpless are the true gold mines of a culture.

— Abraham J. Heschel

Chapter 1

How It All Started

January mornings are cold in North Carolina, especially at three o'clock AM. Dad and I had gotten up at that time to get him ready to go for his triple bypass surgery. We hoped that Mom would be all right until her caretaker came around seven or eight; she was sound asleep, so we left trusting that all would be well.

The waiting room at Rex Hospital was very quiet at five o'clock. There were a few people whom we assumed were there for the same reason Dad was—to get prepped for an early morning elective surgery. There was nothing to do at that moment but sit and wait for him to be called. My mind raced with many thoughts. The one I tried to avoid—but of course couldn't—was that this might actually be the last time I would see him.

Open-heart surgery is serious at any age, but with my dad's eighty-five-year-old heart that had not been doing well for many years, it was especially worrisome. I turned to him. "Dad, are you afraid you might die?"

He shook his head. "No, no, no," he answered. "What I'm worried about is who's going to take care of your mother." There was no recrimination in that sentence; he knew I couldn't quit my job to stay home to care for her. I don't even think he was referring to the fact that Mom and I had not been getting along so well the last few years; he was really just concentrating on her and who was going to take care of her.

Of course, that added a new concern for me. Who *was* going to take care of her? I certainly couldn't do it, but we didn't have the money to do anything else. Mom and I were at a difficult point, but I sure didn't want to see her in a Medicaid nursing home. What would happen if Dad didn't survive the surgery?

It was a long day of waiting. Dad's surgeon came out to greet me. His surgery took the longest—no surprise there. I sat all morning as surgeon after surgeon came in to tell various families that everything was just fine, no problems. Everyone was getting happier and happier as I waited for my dad's surgeon to come out. As time passed into the afternoon, new people started sitting in the waiting room. These were people who were there for emergency surgeries: the burst appendix of a teenager, an old man's heart attack, and so forth. The surgeons were not as positive when they came out of those surgeries. I don't remember anyone actually dying, but the news just wasn't as clearly positive. A man the same age as my dad had been golfing that morning and had had a heart attack. He had been brought in for the same exact reason that Dad had—to have those bypasses on an eighty-five-year-old heart. The man never came out of his coma.

However, my dad—God bless him—made a great recovery. He stayed in the hospital for only five days. I knew hospital stays were drastically shorter than what they used to be, but five days seemed quite brief for an eighty-five-year-old man with what ended up being a quintuple bypass.

I was also relieved because I'd had to take off days from work to stay home to care for Mom while Dad was recovering in the hospital. When I picked him up from the hospital, he was a little nervous of course. He had his big red pillow that he held next to his heart whenever he stood up or sat down. But once he got home and started fixing Mom her meals, doing normal daily chores, and getting back into his old routine, he felt fine. I just assumed things would go back to the way they had been and would stay like that forever.

I came home one day, walked into their apartment, and saw Dad turning Mom's mattress over. This was about a week and a half after the surgery. "Dad, is that heavier than a milk carton?" I asked, reminding him of doctor's orders. He mumbled, "Well, I can't continue to be lazy the rest of my life." I smiled. It was so like my dad; spending three weeks recovering from heart surgery without doing major work—to him that was *lazy*. Of course, I convinced myself that this was the way it was going to be forever.

Dad cared for Mom for three more years. She continued to get worse and she needed more help. She started soiling herself, which he never discussed; he always cleaned up after her with no complaint.

We never thought about hiring some help for him; it just didn't occur to us. Dad had always done his own work himself. During the twenty years they had run small-town newspapers, they occasionally had some employees, but there were also long stretches when they did everything by themselves. He didn't see why he couldn't do that now. And I wasn't thinking ahead, so I thought the same thing.

The challenges continued to mount. Mom was agoraphobic and wouldn't go out to the doctor. Thus, the one thing Dad *would* allow was to have a doctor come to the house. I heard a radio advertisement for an organization called Doctors Making House Calls. Terrific. I talked to Dad about that and he called. The small extra cost was worth paying to have a doctor to the house to give her medication. That turned out to be a godsend, not only because of the doctor, but also because these wonderful people were the ones who got Dad to start to build a small support team.

They arranged to have a nurse come in once a week to check her vitals and well-being. Then they arranged to have hospice come.

After Mom died, I had Dad for another five glorious years. But he started to fail and become weaker. Since I was blind to what was going on with Dad taking care of Mom, I was more clueless than I should have been about what I was going to be facing those last couple of years with Dad—but I wouldn't have done it differently then or now. I'm very glad I kept Dad at home. But I had so much to learn about what to do, what I needed, and what he needed that I just wish I'd had somebody to help me figure some of this out.

I felt so alone.

Chapter 2

You Are Not Alone

The statistics are staggering. Baby boomers are aging. I was born in 1948, the third year of what was called at the time the *postwar baby boom*. Soldiers were coming back from World War II, many having been away for as long as four years. When they came back from the wars with the help of Veterans Administration they obtained mortgages, education and a renewed sense of optimism.

And they started making babies—babies who grew up and are now aging. Every day, ten thousand Americans turn sixty-five. Many of these senior citizens are taking care of *their* elderly parents.

Nearly seventy-nine percent of those who need long-term care are living at home or in community settings and are not in institutions. Thirty-four million adults—16 percent of our population—provide care to adults who are fifty or older. Some of these caretakers are spouses, some are children, and some are nieces or siblings. Many people are either doing what you're doing now or doing what you're contemplating doing.

Elders represent the fastest growing age group in the United States. It is projected that the population of those seventy-five and older will increase by 70 percent by 2025. By 2020, twelve million older Americans will require long-term care services.

Margo Arrowsmith

Alone in a Crowd

So, yes, there were all these people doing the same thing I was. I knew there were a lot of people doing this, but I didn't know any of them. As I wrote this book, I talked to people about it. So many people came up to me and said, "Oh, I know somebody who's doing that. They could really use your book." But none of these people were connected to each other. I knew people who knew people. I talked with people who knew people who knew people. Yet all of these people were on their own.

I have looked for support groups because who needs a support system more than people who work as caretakers? One of the first things I did was go to www.meetup.com where I found a couple of local groups. And then I looked to see when those groups met. I would have loved to go and talk to people, but most of them weren't meeting at all. This makes sense. People with families who are trying to hold down a job and take care of an elderly adult in the home don't have time to go to meetings.

There are people who do run amazing groups. There are daycare centers for elderly people who need to be taken care of as well as daytime social clubs for those who just want company. Many of these places are wonderful, but they don't really help the caretaker with their issues.

I knew I wasn't alone, but I had no idea of the staggering number of people who were doing what I was doing. I also felt isolated, like I was in my very own prison; I had chosen it, though, so I didn't want to complain. I didn't want to complain partly because if Dad had ever heard that I was unhappy, he would have packed his bags and been in a Medicaid nursing home in two minutes. His biggest worry was that he was a burden to me.

It really wasn't true. For the most part he wasn't a burden; he was a joy. That's not to say that there weren't burdens at all because, yes, there were—but I couldn't complain about them. I couldn't complain about them to Dad because although he wouldn't necessarily have packed up and left, he certainly would have felt horrible. I didn't want to talk to anyone about it. I didn't want to talk to any of his doctors, as the first thing out of their mouths would have been, "Well, then it's time for him to go into assisted living or a nursing home." Friends were sweet and understanding, but it was hard to talk to them about it. They all thought I was a saint for taking care of him, so telling them about the burden part would have only reinforced something that I didn't think was true. Yes, it was nice to hear people marvel, "You're so wonderful," but it really didn't make me feel any better. Nobody really understood very much about what I was doing; I felt so alone.

Of course, I also thought if I didn't really talk about it, it wasn't really happening. Thirty years of being a family therapist—you would think I would have known better than that. However, the words *therapist heal thyself* come to mind. Yes, I had spent thirty years helping other people solve their problems, and I was very good at it. But that just wasn't supposed to apply to me.

However, when you are taking care of an elderly parent, that is not the time to stand alone in the crowd. Rather, it's the time to reach out to talk to people, to find people who really do understand as well as some who will help you.

One day Dad was in the hospital. It had happened before, but this particular time he was suffering from pneumonia that caused hallucinations—making him a little difficult to deal with in the hospital. Dad was usually the greatest patient in the world; all the nurses loved him. But this time was different. The nurses who could not spend one-on-one time with him had tied him to a chair. I had no other option but to spend the day in the hospital with him.

That was the first time I reached out to a friend. I asked my friend Lisa to go sit with Mom, and of course she did it. There I was with Dad—trying to keep him safe, talking with him, and trying to do some reality orientation. At the same time I had to deal with the nurses. I was trying to do all of this all by myself because, well, that's what I did. That is what I thought I had to do.

I wasn't too worried that my plans for the day had changed; that had happened before and I thought it was just for a day, but it turned out to be much more than that. Dad spent some time in rehab, and I went back and forth between my house and the hospital—keeping Dad's rule of not leaving Mom alone for more than a half an hour at a time. I still wasn't worried. After all, my dad had had quintuple bypass surgery at age eighty-five; he would just spring right back, right? But it was really just the beginning, and I had no idea what I was getting into.

If you don't know where you're going you will probably end up somewhere else.

— Lawrence J. Peter

My grandfather Orval Byrd took care of his wife Alberta Parr Byrd, until he couldn't, then Mom and Dad took care of them. I just always assumed I would do the same thing and I did.

Chapter 3

Know Where You Are Going

The first things you need to ask yourself are, *Why am I doing this? And where do we want to go?*

I had lots of reasons for caring for Mom and Dad at home. At this particular point, I had an eighty-five-year-old bungalow; we used to laugh because it was the same age as Mom and Dad, and of course Dad was the one who had done most of the renovations. About twenty feet away in my backyard was what had been a 750-square-foot garage; it had two stories with two big picture windows that overlooked a grove of trees. We had converted it into a *mother-in-law unit*. That was my idea, so it would be easier if I needed to care for them. I had my privacy, and I wouldn't have to travel far to see them if they needed anything. Besides, Dad did all the work anyway.

When I was looking for a house after moving to Raleigh, Dad and I did all the real estate shopping together. He was very respectful. Obviously, it was my decision, but he was interested and it was a chance for him to get out and about; he enjoyed the process, and I enjoyed having him there. The house I found and loved had that detached garage. My first comment was, "Dad, if you and Mom ever need any help, we could make this into an apartment and you guys could live here." He didn't like that idea, and I naively assumed that they wouldn't really need care. But it just seemed like the natural thing to do. I thought at the time that I was preparing for what might — but what probably wouldn't — happen.

Mom and Dad took care of her parents as much as they could; of the five children she was the one who was going to do it. When Grandpa could no longer take care of Grandma after her stroke, they moved to the same Iowa town where we lived. Mom found a nice little apartment for them where she was able to pop in on them two to three times a day. They were near downtown where Mom and Dad's business was; that worked pretty well for awhile.

Early in my career I had worked in an intermediate care center with elderly people. I had also worked in nursing homes. I knew enough about these places — even though some of them weren't bad — to know that I certainly didn't want my parents in any of them.

I had a vague idea of why I would do what Mom did for her parents. I didn't like the alternatives, but the idea I had was, *I'll just be there to help*. It wasn't very well thought out.

The Fantasies

Before you decide what you're going to do, you have to understand what your fantasies are about — and be clear, you *do* have them. Just as you had fantasies about your marriage before you married or fantasies about parenthood, you have fantasies about your aging parents.

Perhaps you'll recognize some of these fantasies, perhaps not. Perhaps you have a few of your own that aren't listed here, but take a look and see if you recognize any.

1. I will be the angel of mercy and will finally be the grownup around here.

2. Mom is finally going to appreciate me for who I am and think that I'm okay.

3. I will finally be the favorite child.

4. I will have time with my dad—time I always wanted to have.

Some of these things may happen, but you still need to recognize and understand your expectations.

Okay, so what are <u>your</u> fantasies? Get a piece of paper and write down your fantasies—all of them. The only rule here is to write them down no matter what. Put them on a separate sheet of paper. You want to be able to show this book to somebody else—hopefully your parents. But write them down—all of them.

Be gentle with yourself; smile. When you write down how you might be this great Florence Nightingale, a wonderful person whom even you would admire, *smile*. Do not judge yourself.

Oh, yes, and write down the nightmares, too. Write down your worst nightmare about doing this, as this is part of the fantasies. We can work with the nightmares. Nightmares are really just messages to you, and *daymares* can be worked like dreams; you can learn from them. But don't worry about it now; just write it down. To get you started, I will seed you.

1. I will never ever, ever, ever again have another minute to myself.

2. I will have to quit my job, go broke, and lose the house.

3. I will lose all of my friends, as I will never get to see any of them and they will all give up on me.

Okay, now look at your paper and take all your nightmares to their furthest conclusion. That is important because it often makes nightmares look so ridiculous that you really can laugh at them. *I will lose all my friends and get forty-five cats. Eventually the cats will devour me, and they will find a skeleton three months after I die.* This is gruesome, but also ridiculous. Know that it doesn't have to happen that way and laugh at it.

Remember that some of these nightmares are going to be more realistic than others, but seeing them on a piece of paper is part of starting to make a plan on how to control them. We have to know what they are before we can make a plan.

Enjoy getting rid of the silly ones and have a good laugh over them. But the ones that are more realistic keep noted, as we go through this book, especially the chapters about letting go and organizing a team, because these notes are going to help you do both of those things.

Learn what the realities are because there are going to be a lot of them.

There will be commonalities with the realities—and diversity. Both of these will be helpful to everyone. You learn by seeing how people handle problems similar to yours and also by seeing how they handle problems that are different.

1. Money: You will need to know how much money you're going to have available. You will also need to know how much money a parent has. That includes Social Security and other money they have available. Do they have a long-term care policy? Do they have savings? You'll need to know what their expenses are going to be. If they move into your house, that will free up any rent money to use for care. Be sure to be respectful of them when getting this information. You only need to know the basics; they do need to have privacy.

2. Medical issues: You must have knowledge of your parents' current medical issues. This helps you know what kind of team you need now, and it helps you know what you're looking for in the future. It helps you know what you might need to change in their apartment or in your house.

3. Living arrangements: Assess their living area. Whether it's your home or a place where they are still on their own, you need to assess it. If they're going to live with you, you need to know where you're going to put them, how they're going to have privacy, how *you* are going to have

privacy, and how other family members in your house are going to deal with this.

If your parents are going to stay in their own house, you need to know what you can do to make it safer for them. For example, when my parents were in the garage, it was two stories, and when they first moved in they had a bedroom upstairs. When Mom couldn't climb the stairs anymore they moved the bed downstairs. Dad still used the upstairs, which actually became kind of a sanctuary for him. But that's the kind of thing you will need to assess. If they are going to be moving into your house, you need to know if there is something you can do to make a bedroom downstairs. When I looked for the place I'm living in now, I made sure I didn't look at any house that did not have a downstairs bedroom. I once worked with a woman who converted the downstairs dining room into a bedroom for her father. She and her husband didn't have children, so they just made curtains over the dining room arch; they didn't make a lot of structural changes to the house. However, if they had had children, they might have wanted to build an actual door.

If your parents are going to live on their own, you might want to look into a new place for them, perhaps an apartment close to you, certainly something on one floor. Even if they can climb stairs now, they may not always be able to.

    4. Help: Assess what help is available now. Right now you might not need any, but help can also include company. Your parents might be able to take total care of themselves, but they may need social outlets. What is available nearby? Are there clubs? What volunteer work might they enjoy? Don't be pushy; you can't force them, but know what is available to suggest to them.

Knowing these things will help you avoid the biggest mistakes. Not being prepared, I almost made a huge, expensive, and disastrous mistake.

It happened after Dad's pneumonia. As I mentioned above, he was hallucinating floridly when the pneumonia was very bad. While he eventually made a full mental recovery, we weren't sure he would during the weeks when he was still slow and tentative. I was in a panic. I, of course, had depended on Dad to take care of Mom. I couldn't take off from work to do it. I certainly couldn't take care of the two of them.

I had expected Dad to come home after his pneumonia and be fine. Even though I had spent the entire day with him seeing what terrible shape he was in — with his florid hallucinations — I expected him to come home and be up and running as he had after the heart surgery. This time was different; he was hospitalized for a week and he had a week of rehab after that. Frankly, we didn't know at the time if he was going to recover enough to be able to take care of anyone on his own.

It all happened so fast, and of course I was unprepared; I panicked. My brother came out and we looked at assisted living homes. We discovered some unpleasant truths about these places that look so good from the outside.

The one we found was fairly near to my house; they would let my dogs come and visit my mother. That made it better than the other places. At one place, they insisted my mother go to the dining room for her meals, even though she was agoraphobic. We tried to explain to them about Mother's condition, and that my father — who really didn't need one of these places — would be more than happy to get her meals and take them to her room, so that none of their staff would be inconvenienced. "No," the woman said, "she must come to the dining room." My brother and I just looked at each other and marked that one off. That was disappointing because this was one of the almost affordable ones.

The one we really wanted was of course the most expensive. We talked to a guy behind a desk who wouldn't want to be called a salesman. They were going to get one room with a large bathroom and three meals a day. Snacks were available in the day room. That did not include any care that Mother needed. Although Dad would have supplied that care, they were still going to charge extra for the care they assessed she would need. They were also going to charge double because Dad was going to be there, even though he wouldn't have needed any care at that time.

We did a quick calculation and realized that if Mom and Dad moved there, their money would be gone in eighteen months. Every penny they had saved in their lives would be gone, and of course all of their Social Security would be used to pay for this also. I naïvely said, "So then I guess when the money is gone then Medicaid will take over and they'll pay you." The man smiled and said, "Oh, no, we don't take Medicaid. When their money is gone they will have to find a place that will." That would have meant coming back to me with no money for any care at all.

Then with a smile on his face he said—and he wasn't the only one of these directors who said this,"The biggest mistake that most people make is that they don't come to places like ours until they need them." Now I couldn't help but wonder, *Why would anybody want to live in one room for thousands of dollars a month, depleting their life savings, if they didn't have to?* I have heard from a friend of mine that some people go on cruises because it costs less than assisted living, but they get the same—or even better—services. I didn't say it out loud, as we thought we needed this guy, but I still think it's a good question and would like to hear an answer.

There were other benefits, but the only one that really appealed to me was that Dad would be able to go out for more than half an hour at a time because he wouldn't have to worry about Mom being home alone; that would have been really nice. They thought that it was wonderful, of course, that they had social activities. Well, I guess bingo, one movie night, and all the other activities would have been great, except that Mom wouldn't go and Dad wouldn't have liked it.

I hear there are some wonderful assisted living homes. Then there are some that aren't so great. But if you are thinking about this, one of the things you should do is go into the dining room when they're having a meal. They will all show you a beautiful dining room with nice menus and decent to good food. But in every one of them—and this includes the nicest one we saw—you could hear a pin drop in the dining rooms during meals. There was no chatter, no laughing, and no conversation. People sat with others or alone, but there was no talking. This is more meaningful than a schedule of bingo and movies. There are assisted living places that have lovely social programs; you could probably find one where people chat in the dining room about this, that, or the other thing. But if you really want to know what it's going to be like living in a particular place, look at the dining rooms *during* a meal.

I was scared, and Dad was not back to normal, so we got him to sign the papers and we were ready to go. What we were signing up for was a year and a half in a place that wasn't ideal and would present a huge problem at the end. My parents would be back with me without a dime to spend on any care. Of course, I didn't think that far ahead because I had no plan, and I was scared. *I had no idea that for much less money we could have gotten people to help at home.*

Had we gone through with this, Mom would have been in worse shape in a year and a half, and she would have needed more help than Dad could have given, but there would have been no money. And, of course, after Mom died, there would have been no money to help us care for Dad. There would have been no money for Doctors Making House Calls or anyone to help me with Dad. I knew I wouldn't have wanted him in a Medicaid nursing home.

My brother figured we didn't have a choice, but thanks to Mom we were saved. Due to her diabetes and internal bleeding, my mother's mind was nowhere near as sharp as it had been, but she smelled something in the air and was not having any of it. It was Mom who said no go and saved us all from a huge mistake. Dad was temporarily unsure of himself, so we had talked him into it, but thankfully Mom broke the spell. All he had to hear was her saying no; he loved her so much he couldn't do anything to make her unhappy. Thank you, Mom, *thank you*. Not only did you make your last years better by saying *no*, but also you set the stage that helped me make Dad's last years good.

Know Thyself

I didn't really know what was going on or what I could do, and I almost made a huge mistake. It all happened so fast. One night Dad was okay, and the next morning he was in a fetal position on the floor. The day after that he was in the hospital hallucinating. I never thought something like this would happen—or at least I never *seriously* thought it would—so I had no idea what I was going to do. I almost did the wrong thing.

This is why it's important to think about these things now. A big part of that is knowing who you are in all this and not letting the situation overtake you.

I am going to confess my dirty little secret, a part of who I am. It was one of the reasons I didn't want Dad to go to a home, and it had more to do with *me* than with him. It was one of the reasons I held on in his last year. I was getting a lot of pressure to put him in an assisted living or nursing home. Dad's main visiting nurse loved him very much. She thought that it would be best for him, but I knew it wouldn't. I knew he would hate it. She was determined, but I wouldn't let it happen.

Here's the dirty little secret; this is part of the reason I would not let Dad go to a home. This was something I would not confess to him, something that I really did not want to confess to very many people, if anyone. It was really very selfish.

But first let me tell you the good reasons. I knew Dad was saying he wanted to go, and he was giving his nurse the impression he wanted to go, but I knew my dad; I knew he said this because he felt like he was being a burden to me. He wanted to relieve me of that burden. I also knew that he didn't like being around old people. He was still friends with high school classmates, but the friends my parents made through the years were always years or even decades younger. I had tried to get him to go to a senior club and took him to one, but he thought there were too many old people. He didn't really want to live among them.

Margo Arrowsmith

My dirty little secret is that it would have been more of a burden to have him in assisted living, as I would have had to go visit him. I had choices at home; some nights I came home and I would go into the room where he had his TV and I'd spend hours chatting with him. If there was a football game on, we would jump up and down and scream and holler and carry on like we always did. If there were just a good show or movie on we wanted to watch, we would watch it together.

There were nights I came home and spent the night with him silently working on my computer, something I couldn't have done when visiting. Some nights I came home, peeked in the door, asked Dad how he was doing, and then I'd go upstairs. If he needed anything, he called me.

In assisted living or a nursing home none of that would have been possible. Every day of my life, I would been haunted by the idea that I really should have gone to the home to see Dad that night. I would have known for a fact that he was there, feeling lonely and miserable. I would have felt guilty if I didn't go, and I would have hated it if I had gone.

Conversely, Dad would have missed me; he would have really wanted the company. He didn't like old people. My dad was ninety-two, and his best friend in those last years was forty-five years old. He would have had no interest in making new friends who were over sixty. He would not have made friends in a nursing home. He wanted company, but he wanted one-on-one company with younger people. If he had lived in a home, his friend Rose would have visited one night a week, and I would have needed to go the rest of the week.

And when I was there, I would not have been able to work on the computer. We would have had to be much quieter while watching games and change our habits. I didn't want him in a home for many good reasons, but the selfish one was that it was easier for me to have him home.

That came not only from knowing him, but also from knowing myself.

I knew he didn't want to be surrounded by old people he hadn't known for years; I knew I wanted to come home and have three choices for being with him. Neither of us would have been happy with him in an assisted living home. Some people love it, but we are not those people.

For us, the scenario would have been that all day long I would have dreaded going to the home, and if I didn't go I would have felt guilty. Dad would have been in the home thinking, "I want Margo to come to see me because I'm so lonely, but I really don't want to impose on her." And when I was there we would have been limited to institutional behavior—being quiet while watching a football game, for example. Politely watching a football game is better than not watching it, but it was so much better at home.

And this day would have been very different, of course.

One evening, I came home to spend the night upstairs doing some work. I went down a couple of times to see if Dad was okay; he was. He had decided to sleep in his lift recliner, something he did a lot; it made it easier to go to the bathroom. At 10 p.m. he called me down. He had decided to go to his bed and needed some help. I helped him unbutton his shirt and get into bed. We hugged and said, "I love you."

The next morning I woke up and hung around upstairs for about an hour watching TV, relaxing before I began my Saturday activities. I went downstairs, knocked on Dad's door, and hearing no answer I went in to check on him and say good morning, as I had many times before. It was instantly clear to me that he was gone. There had been so many mornings when he was so still I'd actually get close enough to see if he was breathing. But when he was actually gone, I knew—even standing at the door in a good-sized bedroom with the bed on the far side. When life is gone from a human body there is a stillness like no other. My last memory of him would always be us hugging and saying, "I love you." Had he been in a home, it would have been a call from a nurse with me feeling guilty about the night before.

The house was soon filled with EMTs, the coroner, and the police. I had called Dad's best friend Rose before I called them, so she was there with me. I had been so afraid there would be a circus, but they were all lovely. A police officer later told me how impressed he was that the men from the cremation society who had come to get Dad's body had been so respectful of him.

Had he been in a nursing home, I would have gone there the night he died and wanted to leave, or he would have felt guilty for making me be there. Or I wouldn't have gone at all. Regardless, the next morning I would have gotten a call from some nurse saying,

"Your dad passed in the night." But what I got— and what I will always have—is that memory of giving him a hug of having him hug me back and telling each other, "I love you." That was our last moment together.

If You Are Thinking of Assisted Living

This book is about how to keep your parents home when they are aging and need care. I am an advocate for that solution and a guide for how to do it. Frankly, I'm not an advocate of assisted living, but I think it's fair to mention it because it's an option, especially if you have some money—well, especially if you have a lot of money. But that isn't what this book is about.

However, you need to go through the pros and cons, based on who you are and who your parents are, to make the correct decision for you and yours.

You should go through a *pros and cons* list even if you've already decided what you're going to do. Do this even if you have decided to put them in assisted living, or even if you have decided to keep them at home.

1. **Socialization.** Socialization is a pro for assisted living, but that wasn't going to happen for my dad, so it couldn't go on the pro side. However, this might be a big plus for *your* parents. Your parents may not be as averse to meeting new people their own

age as Dad was. Your parents may love it, and that would be a pro of course. But if that is an important reason for them, don't just look at the schedule. Go to the dining room during meals. Ask to see a bingo night.

2. **Cost.** What does it cost? Ask all the questions about the hidden costs. As I mentioned earlier, the assisted living home we were considering was going to be around two thousand dollars a month for my parents. But that only covered the room and food, and probably bingo. It did *not* cover any medical care. In our case, even though Dad would have been handling all the care, they were still going to charge according to what they assessed Mom would need. Find out about every charge, everything it's going to cost.

3. **Convenience.** Will it really be more convenient for you? This is a place where you want the pro and con list. As I've explained above, it really would *not* have been more convenient for me, but there were times when him living at home was inconvenient. When I wanted to go visit my grandchildren, it would have been nice to not have to find someone to stay with him. However, that is what I had to do. One is a pro and one is a con. Know what yours are and put them on paper.

Put *all* of your issues on paper. You may have more than those three. Put them down, pros and cons. Be sure to put them on paper, as keeping lists in your head really doesn't work.

One thing you want to be very clear about is reading all of the policies of the facility. Read every single one.

The people who tried to encourage me to go the assisted living route—from family to Dad's nurse—talked about how much more care he would get. There would always be someone there. But I am not sure that would be true of people who spend a lot of time in their room. Toward the end, we had a woman who came to the house three times a day for an hour or more, and I was home most evenings. Even if I went out on a particular evening and stayed out all night, Dad knew how to reach me. His friend, Rose, was there one evening every week for his social time. I asked, "Is he really going to get that much attention in an assisted living home?" I didn't think so.

This story is important to let you know just how critical it is to read all the policies and know them well.

After Dad died I read this story out of Bakersfield, California. In March 2013, a registered nurse from a facility called 911 about an eighty-seven year old woman who had stopped breathing. The 911 tape was chilling. The nurse called 911 and the operator said, "Okay, we're sending somebody right over. Now you need to do CPR." The nurse responded that it was against company policy for anyone to do CPR. On the 911 tape you can hear the operator starting to get frantic. "No, you *have* to do CPR we can't get there in time." The nurse calmly insisted that is was against company policy; she wasn't allowed. The woman died, of course. To be fair, when I read follow up reports, it turns out that the children had no complaints. They were fine with the nurse's inaction and the company policy. You need to decide if that is okay with you. You need to know all the policies.

If you're thinking of putting your parent in an assisted living facility, don't assume they will do everything possible to take care of your parent. Ask what they do, what they don't do, and how much the extras will cost. You may be able to get better care for less money at home. Even round-the-clock in-home care may be less expensive than an assisted living home, and Mom will have more one-on-one care.

You want to consider your family fortune. I know this is something that no one likes to admit in the open to anyone else, but we all kind of like a little bit from Mom and Dad when they go; at least most parents want to have some to give. When I started to work with Dad to assemble his support team to make sure he was going to be well taken care of at home, one of his biggest concerns was, of course, money. He grew up poor before the Depression, and then his family lived *through* the Depression. He did not squander money. We needed to convince him that getting a nurse to come in three times a day to help him with his needs was not squandering money. He was afraid that if he spent all his money, he would have nothing left if he had to go to a home.

I reminded him that if he had gone to an assisted living facility with Mom, all of their money would have been gone in less than two years; going into a nursing home would have made his money go even faster. I explained to him that he would actually spend less money if hiring a couple of people could keep him home.

He also wanted money left over to leave to his kids. Convincing him that this wasn't important was very hard. He had looked forward to that for many decades. Whether it's your folks who want to leave you money — or you who want it — I am not judging. Just understand that there is likely to be more of it with a team who can keep Mom or Dad at home. Remember that while hiring a team can be cost effective, you must also be wise about where you spend the money and in finding volunteer sources.

A team will cost something, but don't try to do it alone. That is when you will hate the job, resent it, have to quit work, and you may just give up and send them away.

You can't do this alone, folks

You have to make a team. I will talk about this more in the Love Formula part of the book, which is probably the most important section. *You have to make a team.* To quote Hillary Clinton, "It takes a village." Yes, she was talking about raising children — but trust me — it takes a village to take care of your aging parents. It takes a village to give them everything they need, and it takes a village for you to be able to not just survive the experience but to actually *thrive* and be able to enjoy the time, so that you can forever say you are glad you did it.

You need to build a community that can do for you what you are doing now. We need to find people who can do what you really don't want to do, so you can enjoy what you *do* want to do.

Margo Arrowsmith

You also need to have another community to which you can vent and complain. You can't really talk about the burdens to your parents' team, but you can do it with people who are in a similar situation and know what it's like. You need people who can vent and laugh with you. You need a community of people who know that even with the complaining, you really still do want to do this. You need a community of people who will listen to your joys and still know that what you're doing is hard.

Chapter 4

The LOVE Formula

My LOVE formula can get you through caring for your aging parent with joy and without unnecessary sacrifice. I developed this formula based on my thirty years of doing therapy and problem-solving counseling with hundreds of individuals and families, combined with my ten years of involvement with elder care at home.

The first part of the formula is to learn to let go.

You will learn to let go of the past, or at least the parts of it that are holding you back today.

You will learn to let go of your expectations of who your parents are supposed to be today.

Perhaps most importantly, you will learn to let go of who you think you're supposed to be. Note that I didn't say let go of *who you are*, but rather whom you *think* you are supposed to be during this time.

The next step is to organize.

This refers to building your team, of course. You will learn to make a team of people who are going to do what you don't want to do—or can't do. That way you will be free to do for your parents what brings you joy while being able to live your life, keeping your job and friends. This team will add value to the experience for both you and your parents. Some of the team members will be paid, some will be volunteers, and some may be both. I'm going to help you learn how to find these people. The team is going to make your parents safer and happier and let you keep your life.

The next step is to learn to value *your parents and who you are.*

Appreciate and find value in who your parents are and what they can do now. Appreciate them for what you will learn from them in this journey. This is going to help them feel better about who they are and their situation, and it's certainly going to make it a lot easier for you.

You also need to learn to value yourself, for what you can do, not what you should do.

The fourth step is to do periodic evaluations. Take a few minutes to be clear about what is working and what isn't. When you are clear about where you are, you can tweak things so that this beautiful machine of a team will keep going right up to the end.

During this time you will also evaluate yourself in terms of your own aging process. Taking care of elderly parents tells you a lot about how you want to age. You can learn a lot during this time about how to make your own aging the best it can be. Taking care of the elderly can scare you about the future; it can also teach you important lessons for yourself.

These pages for notes as you read. Be careful about writing things you wouldn't want others to read, put that on a separate sheet.

Margo Arrowsmith

Chapter 5

How On Earth Did I Get Here?

Dad's Pneumonia

I don't know how Mom managed to make the call. Dad got out of the house less and less toward the end of her life; he wouldn't leave the house any longer than half an hour, and that was to rush to the grocery store and back.

Part of the problem was that he couldn't teach Mom how to use the phone. Because of internal bleeding, she went through periods of dementia. At one point she had been the editor-in-chief of three different newspapers while running other volunteer organizations. She had been a dynamo, but right now Dad couldn't even get her to use a telephone. He had bought a beeper and a cell phone for himself–things he really didn't want–hoping that he could teach her how to just press that automatic dial button so that if she needed anything she would get him, but it never worked.

This morning, however, the phone rang–thankfully. I think I was in bed at the time but awake. I heard Mom's panicked voice. "Come over. You must come over. You've got to come over." I went outside and crossed a few feet over into their house, and there was Dad lying on the floor in a fetal position.

I called the EMTs, and soon the house was filled with the usual people for having medical emergencies, including the firemen with the fire trucks outside. I used to laugh and say they should have called it the *EMT Circus*, but we were pretty used to all of that by this time; they had been there so many times for Mom. Now I was more worried about Dad.

They put Dad on his bed. By this time he could talk a little bit and his vitals were okay. He really didn't seem himself, but he was able to talk. They asked him questions, and he could answer them. They asked him if he wanted to go to the hospital, and he said no. There I was in my delusions. I did want him to go to the hospital because I was a little worried. I was confident that he would come home the next day good as new.

Too often in life we forget the things we should remember and remember the things we should forget.

–Anonymous

You will find that it is necessary to let things go, simply for the reason that they are heavy. So let them go, let go of them. I tie no weights to my ankles.

–C. JoyBell C.

The first wave of Byrd grandchildren. I am in the back.

Our first years are filled with connections and experiences not of our choice. It is important to sort it out, keep what is gold or silver, learn from what you can, but then let go of the garbage that is holding you back, making you suffer.

Chapter 6
Let Go

You, like everyone else in the world, will come to parent care with the baggage of your past; your parents are going to have some of their own. The first step is to acknowledge this and do your best to eliminate yours. Trying to hide your baggage in the closet just doesn't work, because it will jump out at you at odd times when you least expect it—times when you don't want it and times when you can't control it. Imagine coming home from the gym, taking your clothes and just stuffing them in the back of the closet. Pretty soon you're going to have a smelly closet. You need to get it out, launder it, and make it better, more manageable.

My dad was the easiest guy to get along with. But he had a life long bad habit that made his last years harder for both of us. He always stood while he worked at his printing presses. In his early sixties he had back trouble; the doctor warned him to start sitting. In his mind, people who sat at presses were lazy, so he refused to do it. I was angry at him the first time. The anger at the time was really that I saw him as being vulnerable; it was my first glimpse at his mortality— and therefore at my own.

He continued to stand while working, but he started to feel better so we all stopped thinking about. It would not have helped for me to become obsessed about his aging, but if I had started to grasp a little bit that it was happening, it might have made things a little easier for me down the road.

My first house was a seventy-five-year-old bungalow. It was built the same year Dad was born. He did most of the remodeling, of course. I returned one day from work to find that my new dining room chandelier was hanging. It was July, and it must have been about 150 degrees in the attic. The floor over the dining room was really nothing more than some beams. I chastised him a little bit for doing that all by himself without anybody even being in the house. What if he had fallen? He just said, "Oh well, you wanted it done, and I wanted to do it for you." So again, he was reinforcing my childhood belief that he was always going to be strong, and I went along with it.

The first thing to do is to sort things out; not everything is baggage. Some of it might be resentmentwhich could actually be useful. But you won't know what is useful and what isn't until you look at it. I use an analogy of chains in a jewelry box. It seems that no matter how carefully you put your silver and gold chains in your jewelry box and leave them flat, not touching each other, when you open up the box they will be tangled. The temptation might be to just give up and throw them away, but that would be a mistake. In that mess of tangled chains there might be some brass that really is junk that is dirtying your precious metal and you could get rid of it. But there are also some gold and silver chains, so it really makes sense to sort it all out. Separate them; do the tedious work of untangling them so that you can decide which of these are valuable to you and which aren't.

You may learn that even the baggage or brass that seems to be junk has some value, something they can teach you.

Gather the Clues

My dad was the greatest person in the world. He was kind and patient, and he would do anything for anybody. But he was also stubborn, and sometimes that made me mad. My old feelings about all of this showed up when I took care of him when he was aging.

The first time I ever got mad at my dad was when he was sixty-one years old and beginning to show some physical vulnerability. He was younger than I am now, and the physical vulnerability he was showing is something I don't have now. Even at age thirty, I knew it was something he didn't have to have–so I was angry at him.

It wasn't that he had done anything bad. But at that point he was going against my childhood fantasy that he was always going to be strong; he was supposed to be my buffer against mortality and aging. I thought I had a legitimate reason to be mad at him for having pains in his legs and back. The doctor told him that he had to stop standing when he was at the printing presses. He had gone through his entire life standing at printing presses, thinking that people who sat down while doing their job were lazy. And now here was this doctor telling him that it had caused him problems and he needed to stop. I don't think my anger came just from him not wanting to change the way he had been doing things; *it's that he had the nerve to show that he was a fragile human being.* We even get baggage from the best parents.

There were other things that could have reared up from the past. For example, Mom and Dad never missed a performance or event that my brother was in, but they missed lots of mine. In time, I forgot about this; I didn't think about it anymore. However, I must confess that there were a couple of times when I'd have to do something like babysit for Mom while Dad was in the hospital, and that little thought would pop into my head, *Well, they never went to my choir performance.* Then I would be embarrassed that those feelings were still down there bothering me. That was one area where having been a family therapist for thirty years actually helped me. I had helped many people accept that, yes, they *still* might have those thoughts.

Even if they don't make any sense and seem petty to an adult, the best thing to do is to acknowledge them and watch them float away. You can learn to do the same · acknowledge them and then watch them float away.

List Your Grievances

Okay, your parents weren't perfect. You know it and I know it; now put it on paper. Again, you might want to make this paper very private, and I am going to emphasize that you really should *never show this to your parents*. There really isn't any point to it; it will only make them feel bad, or make you feel bad. Hurting people is not the point of this exercise. List all your grievances; if they come to mind, they're obviously still there.

Sort Them Out

Some grievances are surprisingly silly, and just putting them on paper will give you a good laugh and help you let them go. Existential psychotherapist Irvin Yalom wrote about a technique for patients' resentment. He had a patient stand in front of a mirror and say over and over, "I will not become a successful businessman until my mother, who has been dead for twenty years, acknowledges that I was a good student." That's pretty darned silly, isn't it? The reason he had the patient repeat that over and over was that eventually it became very funny. It was sad that this guy had felt this way for so many years. That is *exactly* what he felt, but saying it while looking at himself in the mirror enabled him to eventually see just how silly it was; then he was able to laugh about it.

List the Losses

What about your parents' aging makes you mad? This is not the time to judge; it's the time to put it on paper. I have already confessed that Dad's aging forced me to consider my own aging. What are your feelings? Are you angry–even deep down–that they are inconveniencing you? That's a loss, folks, and when you're taking care of aging parents who have daily losses, it's going to be part of what you deal with, so just acknowledge it. It could be something else for you; just let yourself think of what it is.

Use the Lists

Look at your list and take them all to the extreme. Yes, take them all to the ridiculous extreme. "My mother hated my hair when I was in high school, and that's why I have gall bladder troubles now."

We all have resentments, some serious and some silly. If we don't face them they will take over at inconvenient times. This will affect your care of your parents and your life in many other ways. Let yourself really get into this. You can make something funny out of just about everything. If you look at most sitcoms on TV today, most of the things they deal with seem so serious when they occur in life. That is why we enjoy these shows. We are able to laugh at the pains and foibles that seem so serious when they occur in our lives. If only we could learn to transfer that to our lives.

An example is the show *Everybody Loves Raymond*. These people are not nice to each other. They spend most of their days annoying each other or being mean or thoughtless and then getting upset about what the others have done to them. It's really an awful situation, but we laugh. If only we could learn to laugh at these things in our own lives.

Take some of these grievances and losses and make them into a sitcom. *Isn't she funny when she lets Marie get to her?, When she expects things from Raymond that he won't do?* Think about them in a way that makes them funny, because–again–when they are funny and you can laugh at them, they don't control you.

There may be something that you *can't* make funny; look at this more closely. I'm not talking about the very severe cases where fathers sexually abuse their daughters or beat their sons. I doubt if very many of those daughters are considering elder care. Some things happen that no matter what you do or how you stand on your head, you just can't laugh at them. Those need to be looked at more.

Just how angry are you? If caring for your aging parent is too much to handle on your own, you might need to see a counselor about getting help. Later I'll discuss building a support team to help take care of your parents, but somebody that might help take care of *you* can also be part of the team.

What Do You Expect Your Rewards Will Be?

What do you expect to get from taking care of Mom and Dad? We talked about that a little earlier when discussing fantasies. Did you never feel loved and are doing this now because you think that you might finally feel it?

Remember the story of the prodigal son from the Bible? A man has two sons. He gives them both their inheritance while he's alive. One of them stays home and works hard building the business while the other runs off and squanders his money on partying and having a good time–then becomes destitute. Remember what the Bible says about this? When the prodigal son returns, he is given a huge party with the fatted calf. The good son is resentful, but when he complains, the father is surprised. The meaning of this story is that God will always welcome you back to the fold, but there are other lessons to learn here.

That lesson is to let go of the expectations you have for how your parents are going to react to your caregiving. There are good children and bad children. There are children who *think* they are the good children, while there are all sorts of things going on in the kids' minds, such as what that means to the parent. However, parents don't necessarily see it the way we do; they may have a favorite child, and it may not be the one who makes the most sense. It might be the prodigal son.

This jockeying for position is so much a part of the human condition; it becomes the basis for a lot of baggage and expectations. It is not at all unusual that the one who is the favorite or perceived favorite *isn't* the one caring for the parents and shouldering the work. In fact, sometimes the ones who felt *less* care from the parents do the caretaking because they think it's finally their chance to be recognized.

If this is happening with you, understand that you may or may not get the recognition you seek. You need to let go of that expectation. It doesn't mean your reasoning is faulty; nor does it mean you should close up the book, throw it away, and send Mom and Dad packing. But if that is one of your motivations, you just need to understand it so you can put it in perspective and not get destroyed when it doesn't work out the way you wanted it to. You need to let go of the expectations about how Mom and Dad are going to feel about you for doing this.

For much of my caretaking time I actually had both of my parents. Initially, Dad mostly took care of Mom and I was there to help. My relationship with my mother had had its ups and downs through the years, but there were many good years. I have some very fond memories from my childhood. She worked with my father on their newspapers for long hours, but I really don't think I felt neglected. I spent a lot of time actually there with them. Sometimes when I was at home I knew I could call my mom if I got lonely. She stopped doing whatever she was doing to talk with me. The reality–and I think I knew this even when I was a child–is that I was probably better off without having my mom around too much because, well, we clashed.

I loved hearing the following story. My mother always wanted six girls and one boy. Even before she met my dad, she had fantasies about who her daughters were going to be and what kind of a relationship she would have with them. She had been married five years when my brother was born. As the story goes, she was so glad to have a child at that point that she wasn't disappointed. I don't know if my brother ever heard this or how he felt about it, but it meant a lot to me. It was another seven years before I was born. Mom had been in labor with me for almost two days when she woke up from her anesthesia; in those days, they would put women out. When she was told she had had a daughter, her response was, "Don't worry, I love him very much. You don't need to make me feel better. I know I have a boy." She just couldn't believe that she finally got her daughter. And she knew just who I was going to be and what our relationship would be.

Margo Arrowsmith

Like many people of that time, Mom thought that children were blank slates who could be written on, made into the vision of choice. She had dreamed of a little *mini-me* who would talk with her about everything, that somehow the conversations would be just what she had imagined. I was very different from what she had expected, however, and certainly very different from her. Even when we agreed about something such as clothing, any variance in expression on my part often caused her anxiety; she would say something that was basically what people call a conversation stopper. I would stop talking, and she would be upset because she didn't have a daughter who would talk with her.

There were lots of good times, and she also showed pride in something I said that surprised me. She really wanted a good relationship with me, but her expectations and beliefs about what *should* be often got in the way.

As she aged, her bouts of dementia made things worse. Some of it hurt. Sometimes when I was at their house, I'd say something, and she would just kind of shake her head and say, "You are really odd." I think her dementia ruined her ability to filter her thoughts.

One of the nights that Dad was at the hospital, I was again sleeping at their house to care for Mom; she had a bed in the living room, and I was sleeping in the recliner. I wasn't comfortable, and she was unhappy that he was gone. I was especially annoyed as she was crying about how unfortunate she was that she had to spend a night without her husband. I had no patience for this. What I was thinking was, *You spent sixty-nine years with the greatest guy in the world, and you're complaining that you don't have him for one night.* I didn't have much empathy for her; I was tired, uncomfortable, and didn't want to be there—let alone have to listen to her complaining. She was not meeting my fantasy by not recognizing my sacrifice; it was not a good night.

Finally, we went to sleep. At three in the morning I woke up and I looked down; my mother was crawling around on the floor. I called EMS right away. When they came, we discovered that Mom— who was diabetic—had a blood sugar level of forty. That was near death, and before the EMS arrived she was hallucinating. I was trying to get her back into bed with no success when she started a rant. While crawling on the floor, she said over and over, "I love you so much, why do I keep hurting you? I love you so much, why do I keep hurting you?"

It was at that moment I knew that while her inability to communicate with me has affected my life, in that moment I realized that is wasn't about me. It wasn't about my inadequacies; it was about *her*. The tragedy was that this woman who had wanted this great relationship with her daughter for so long had kept stepping on her own toes, shooting herself in the foot so that she could never have the thing she wanted so badly. It was her tragedy.

It was at that moment that I was really able to let go of my resentment of having a mother who kept telling me I was wrong, shaking her head and saying I was odd. The resentment melted away as I realized it wasn't about me. That didn't mean I wasn't sad; I hadn't had the mother I wanted. It still hurts sometimes, but once I let go of that resentment about feeling like I was the problem, it was much easier. Letting go of the resentment made it easier to do what I had to do to take care of her. There was really nothing to be done about it. At that time it certainly wasn't necessary or possible for her to change, but it was easier for me because I'd let go of my resentment of her.

5 Basic Steps for Letting Go of Resentment

Just as grieving has steps, so does letting go of resentments and fantasies. We have to let go before anything new can be born.

It's exciting to watch your children grow, but each new development means we lose something; once a toddler takes his first step, his parents no longer have their crawler. You rejoice in your baby's new ability to walk, but you have to give up what she was just yesterday. This happens with any relationship, even in the best parent-child relationships. You have to be able to grieve in order to let go.

You need to acknowledge that your parents are really just human after all, that the mistakes they made with you–whether they let you down or hurt you–happened because they are human. Sometimes we hold onto resentment because it's easier than letting go of the hope that our parents are more than human.

Developing a caretaking role with your mom and dad means that you're letting go of the relationship you had with them and creating something new. They still deserve respect. They aren't your children, after all, just because you're taking care of them; but you have to let go of what was.

The Five Steps

1. *You must identify the resentment of the loss.*

You have to do this alone, or at least without your parents. It is hard enough for us to acknowledge our resentments to *ourselves* let alone to other people; you might tend to be a little more hesitant with another person around, unless of course it's a professional. Sometimes when we talk to other people they try to jolly us up too soon. They often try to make us feel better before we are ready. You just need to know what you're giving up. Negative things are hard to give up when you've lived with them for so long. That's one of the reasons that it's hard for people to get out of bad relationships. The fantasies are even harder to give up because they were nice. It's very hard to give up the vision of who they were and face what they can't be now.

2. *Grieve*

Don't just shrug and tell yourself to get over it. You *will* get over it, but you're less likely to do it if you shrug it off; you need to go through the process. You are also going to learn a lot about yourself as you try to figure this out, so value the process. Just don't let it go on and on forever. One of the things I suggest is that people set an appointment with themselves to feel bad. It might take a half an hour, it might take an hour, or it might take fifteen minutes a day, but what you do is say to yourself, *I have a lot to do today and I feel fine, but at three o'clock I set an appointment to feel bad until 3:30 p.m. I will feel all those bad things.* I wouldn't go longer than an hour. Play sad music, think the thoughts, and let yourself cry, but remember when the appointment is over, it's over. Stop, and then go on with the rest of your life. If the intensity doesn't begin to decrease after a couple of weeks, I suggest you find a professional to help you. This does not have to mean going into full-scale analysis. Sometimes it can be done with short-term therapy, and sometimes it takes longer.

There are lots of ways to do this: everything from talk therapy to group therapy to behavioral therapy to some of the new types of things such as Emotional Freedom Technique (EFT), something I recommend to a lot of people–or maybe a combination of the above. But remember that when you start to make your team, some of those team people are going to be there not for your parents but for *you*.

3. Compassion

This is what I did with my mother when I realized that her anger at me for not being the daughter she wanted was not about me. Because of her need to control, she was unable to enjoy what she had. That was sad for me, but it really helped me deal with the situation when I understood it, as I was able to have compassion for her. Your parents are not getting old to disappoint you or give you a hard time. That can be one of those things that is embarrassing to think about because in our logical minds we all know that people don't get old to embarrass us or hurt us. In her studies about the grieving process, Elizabeth Kubler Ross discovered that one of the things people often do when they lose a loved one is get angry at the loved one for dying. Unless it's a suicide or something similar, it's very rare that the person died in order to hurt us, but in fact we *feel* that way, and part of grieving is coming to terms with our anger. The reality is that it's your parents who are going through this; *they* are the ones having a harder time walking or having trouble getting to the store. It affects us and hurts us, but it is really their loss. Have compassion for them, but know that does not mean babying them or giving in to everything they want.

4. *Forgiveness*

After compassion comes forgiveness. Forgiveness without compassion doesn't work very well, and it can breed resentment. This is not necessarily something you say to your parents. If I had said to my mother, "Mom, I forgive you for not being able to have a conversation with me," the best I could have expected would have been that she didn't know what I was talking about; the worst would have just made the situation even worse.

If it's something that the two of you have gone over and been fighting about, then perhaps you could say something, but don't expect to be able to control how they answer you. If you apologize to someone, you need to do it just for the sake of your apologizing; you don't want to expect something from them because you're probably not going to get it.

5. *Look for the Lesson, the Positive Part*

Take what you just learned and look for the positive. If your mother was very critical, you may have learned to work harder and become a success. It might have been nicer if she had figured out another way to help you, but the point is that you're doing okay, and it worked out. Find something positive that came from this, because there is something.

Get it on paper. Again, this is just going to be for *you*. This is not something you will be sharing with the world, unless there's a reason to do so. Not sharing it with your mom or dad is a good thing. In fact, you might even want to destroy what you write down. The important thing here is that this is going to move you ahead.

It's possible you'll need more. As I said earlier, you may be able to talk this through yourself, but you may also need a professional to talk to. Even if you just found somebody who could do short term work like EFT or EMDR, something to help you get past whatever's got you stuck. By the way, if you do either one of those two things, be sure to get a trained therapist.

Letting Go Of Your Fantasies About You

You also have fantasies about yourself that will get in the way if not identified.

Get the paper and pencil and list all of the fantasies of your sainthood. Make a list of everything you think you *can* and *should* be able to do. For example:

1. You will handle this all by yourself.

2. You're never going to ask anybody for anything because you're so strong and such a good person.

3. You're not even going to break a sweat.

Or is your fantasy that you will hate doing this and it will destroy you? Or that your friends will all abandon you for not being fun anymore?

My mother taught me a song when I was feeling sorry for myself when I was little. I don't have the tune, but the lyrics went like this:

> *Everybody hates me, nobody loves*
> *me, Guess I'll go eat worms;*
> *Big ones, fat ones, skinny ones, scrawny ones*
> *Gee how they do squirm.*

****

> *Everybody loves me,*
> *Nobody hates me.*
> *Gee, I wish I hadn't eaten all those worms!*

My mother used to make me laugh with that song when I was feeling sorry for myself. I have to confess there are times I sing it today. It's like the reality check I mentioned earlier — make yourself laugh about your worst fantasies. And don't forget to laugh about the Superwoman fantasies.

What Do You Expect From Your Parents?

I fantasized that my mother would start seeing me as a capable individual, separate from her. That didn't happen, but I did get that moment when she confessed that the problem was hers.

My dad was very appreciative of what I did for him and Mom, but he never showed it the way I hoped he would. I had to learn to accept his way of acknowledging me and my work. Had I not done that and held on to the old expectation, I would have been in the same position as the prodigal son's brother, unhappy and not aware of what was coming his way.

Some parents won't appreciate this at all. They might see you caring for them as their due, or they might feel so bad taking advantage of you that they think the best way to protect themselves is to not acknowledge your sacrifices.

What do you expect from your parents about compliance? Do you think they will abdicate all their power to you? Or do you think yours will go to them?

I worked with a woman who was caring for her father who had been in an assisted living home. He called her to say he didn't like it and asked her to come and get him. She did, and she found an apartment for him near her in her large city. She said she was spending a lot of time now doing things for him such as shopping. I suggested she find someone else to do that, but she stated that her father wouldn't like that. Oops—time for some negotiation there. There are ways to do that and I will teach you how. This woman seemed to think that she had to give up everything, even though she had already done a lot by getting her father where he wanted to be.

Fairytale Fantasies

Time for more paper. Write down your fairytale fantasies. Put down the silly ones and the embarrassing ones. All of them. It's important to write it all down. You need to sort it out in order to let go of the impossible ones and to figure out how you can make the important ones come true. This is for your eyes only, so don't hold back.

For example:

1. I will find a new me and learn new strength. (This one will happen, but you have to know about it so you can recognize the real strength and not be disappointed about what can't happen.)

2. This will get me to heaven. (It might, but probably not in quite the way you imagine.)

Margo Arrowsmith

The Nightmares

1. I won't survive this.

2. I will have to give up everything in my life.

3. I will die alone.

Whatever comes up, fantasy or nightmare, take it to the furthest conclusion. It may end up being funny like the worm song, but it may also show you some things that you need to change and how to start a plan to make things better for everyone.

What You Expect of Others

In the next chapter we learn how to make a team, but you need to know what to expect from these people, what is real, and what isn't. You also need to be realistic about who can help you and how, as well as who *can't* help you and why not. You need to let go of what you think they should be doing. That doesn't mean you should pretend; just be realistic.

Siblings

Siblings can be the big elephant in the room. They were the ones who shared your sibling rivalries as you were growing up; they were the ones with whom you were in competition for approval from your parents. They are the ones with whom you are in competition for parental resources of all kinds. You may have even more expectations for them than you did for your parents. Having siblings can be both a joy and a frustration.

The best story I encountered was of two sisters. Both were retired with husbands, and their mother had Alzheimer's. They lived about half an hour away from each other. One of them would take their mom for one week, and then the other one would take her the other week. This way they both contributed equally, and they each had a whole week off. It worked out very well for them. They also had siblings who lived in other cities. When it came time that they could no longer keep her, even on alternating weeks, they found a good home. The others had had the expectation that they would always be there and were upset. They had to let go of this. The two sisters were the ones doing the work and it was their decision.

The worst story that I know of is about a family of six children and their spouses. The mother had Lou Gehrig's disease and had gotten to the point where she could still eat and swallow, but she was basically paralyzed; she could talk a little bit, but it was a strain. The children all decided they wanted to keep her at home. For a long time, one of the brothers was in charge of the care, and the mom got the best. Things went well until he went to do missionary work overseas. A brother-in-law—whose main concern was saving the inheritance—took over, and the care level decreased. Everyone was heartbroken.

Your story is probably somewhere in between, hopefully closer to the story of the two sisters than that of the other family. You can share this book with your siblings and, by the way, with your parents. But I advise you now—don't have expectations about how they're going to react to it.

Use the notes pages for exercises, but remember, these should probably not be shared so use other paper for those items.

Margo Arrowsmith

You Can Keep Your Parents At Home

Margo Arrowsmith

You Can Keep Your Parents At Home

Margo Arrowsmith

Organizing is what you do before you do something, so that when you do it, it is not all mixed up.

— A. A. Milne

The trouble with organizing a thing is that pretty soon folks get to paying more attention to the organization than to what they're organized for.

— Laura Ingalls Wilder

Fitz and Marjorie were married in 1935, the height of the depression. They learned to be thrifty. In 1948 they bought the first of three weekly newspapers and learned to do a lot by themselves. It was a hard sell to get them to agree to spend some of their hard earned cash on a team.

Chapter 7

Organize

Organization is the foundation of care. It will enable you to take care of your parents while keeping your job, your life, and your sanity.

Never forget why you are doing this. Don't get so bogged down by the organizing that you forget to see that your parent is having a good life. Organization is to make things easier, not to run your life.

My dad took care of my mom basically all by himself. He did it for too many years. It had gotten to the point where he could only leave the house for a half an hour at a time, and that would be to go to the grocery store, where he hurriedly got whatever he could buy so that he could rush home before Mom needed him. He wanted to do it this way because he loved her so much, but toward the end it was too much for him. I should have insisted earlier that he get some help, but it just never occurred to me; it certainly never occurred to me to argue with him about it.

Part of his problem with not wanting help was that he didn't want to spend any money. They had gotten married in 1935 in the midst of the Depression; Dad had grown up poor his entire life. He was terrified that if Mom needed to go to a nursing home that he would not have the money to put her there. And of course he was also worried about that for himself.

Margo Arrowsmith

When my parents were in their sixties and probably planning to work the rest of their lives in their own printing shop in San Diego, California, they read a story about a couple in Florida who had saved their whole lives for their retirement. When the retirement came, the woman became very ill with cancer. Their retirement funds were gone. When the woman died, he was left with no retirement money and no life; in despair, he killed himself. Somehow that got in the newspaper, and my dad read it out in California. It was at that time that they decided to sell their business and their house to buy an RV, to spend the rest of their lives traveling around the country. It was a very risky thing for them to do, but they did it for about ten years and enjoyed every minute of it. Eventually, they decided to settle down, and they moved to Raleigh, North Carolina to be near me. They had some money left and again got to be very thrifty.

Dad was now trying to save as much as possible because he wanted to be able to take care of Mom if she needed it, as they had tried to do for Mom's mom and dad. When Grandma and Grandpa were sick there was no Medicaid or Medicare. When the time came that they absolutely had to have more care than Mom could give, the only place they could go in a small Iowa town was pretty dumpy. Dad was haunted by that.

I tried to explain to him that things were different now. Medicare doesn't pay for nursing homes any longer than two months, but there's Medicaid after that. Frankly, and more to the point, they didn't have enough money to be able to keep Mom in a nursing home anyway. It wouldn't have taken long before all of their money would have been gone and she would have had to go on Medicaid · whether he wanted her to or not. What he couldn't see was that paying some money for help would have enabled him to keep her home longer.

I did get him to go out once for my birthday and to take me to a movie. I asked somebody at work if they knew anybody who was interested in babysitting for an adult, and we got a woman to come in for about two and a half hours. She was fine with Mom, and we went out to see *Million Dollar Baby*. On the way back Dad had some tears in his eyes. I asked if it was because she died in the end. He shook his head and said, "No, it was the way her family treated her." Dad was always tenderhearted, which made him a good caretaker, but he was also one who sacrificed more than he had to in order to do a good job.

Mom wouldn't brush her hair. She would let Dad do it, but that wasn't his area of expertise; it had gotten very matted in the back. They did allow a friend of mine to come in and cut it all off because she probably wouldn't have let him or me do it. That experience didn't cost anything and taught me about getting volunteers to help. But Dad was still pretty darned resistant to the whole thing.

Mom also had agoraphobia and would not go to the doctor. She would go to the hospital, but that was often because a whole lot of people from the EMS would come. If you put her in an ambulance she wasn't going to be unpleasant with all those strangers, but neither Dad nor I could get her to go to the doctor. A couple of times when my brother was out from California he and I got her in the car and got her to the doctor. After all this trouble, she met with an M.D. who listened to her heart, looked down her throat, and said, "Okay, that's enough." This same doctor's practice had refused to give my mother medication because they hadn't seen her in the office. It was a little annoying that the two times we went to so much trouble to get her to the doctor's office, that was all they did. I remember asking them,

"If that's all you're going to do, why can't you have a nurse come to the house so that you have her information to give her meds?" They wouldn't do that.

One day I was listening to the radio and heard an advertisement for something called Doctors Making House Calls. My parents and I had grown up in small towns in Iowa. I remembered calling the doctor in the middle of the night and he would actually answer the phone. When I was in high school, my friend Katie's father was a doctor and had the phone next to his bed; he would answer the phone and go out in the middle of the night. A couple of years ago I connected with Katie's sister on Facebook, and I asked her if I was remembering this correctly. "Could it be true that when we were young your father did house calls?" She said, "Yes." She said there were eleven children in the family, and he used to always take one of them with him; that was each child's special alone time with him.

We called Doctors Making House Calls; they took Medicare with a bit of an extra fee for having the doctor come out to the house. Dad agreed that it was reasonable to compensate for the time, as doctors' time is very valuable. He was happy to do this because · even though it involved spending some extra money—he knew it was the only way we could get this done, and of course it was a custom he was used to. Not to mention that we got far more than our money's worth. The doctors were wonderful. They came to the house and gave Mom one of the most thorough physicals I think she ever had in her life. It was certainly much better than what she got from the doctor in the doctor's office.

What is perhaps even more important was that they also talked Dad into some other services—not a lot, and I don't think he paid much, if anything, for them. I was not involved in his finances, but I know that services were covered by Medicare. The weekly nurse was paid by Medicare once they did the work to qualify Mother based on her condition. The nurse also helped Dad understand her medications and make sure that he was administering them properly. There were other things added in, not the least of which was how important it was to both of them to have another adult in the house; there were social benefits.

Toward the end of Mom's life, they noticed that Dad was really starting to have a rough time. They saw it better than I did. It was this organization that made that most important connection, even though none of us thought that Mom was near death. In many ways, she was actually healthier than Dad was. She had had some surgery due to bleeding from a few major places in her body; those were treated, but other than that and her diabetes, in many ways she was healthier than Dad.

I'll never forget the day I called Dad from work and he was cross with me. My dad was hardly ever short-tempered; he certainly was never cross on the telephone, but he was cross with me that day. When I got home that night he was very apologetic. I found out what happened. Mother had started having troubles with her functions and was soiling herself. I often came home at night; he'd be down on his hands and knees on the carpet. He was past eighty-five at this point, and he was cleaning brown spots off the carpet. I said nothing to him, as he clearly did not want to talk about it. That particular day she had soiled herself in bed. He'd gotten her all cleaned up and in her chair and would not have complained about it until he went to change the sheets on her bed and realized that he had been so stressed and busy taking care of her the last few days that he had not done any laundry. He did not have clean sheets. It was at that moment that I called him, that moment when he was feeling like such a failure. He had let down his bride and was angry with himself.

That was just a little bit after Doctors Making House Calls had referred us to hospice. As I said earlier, we thought Mom was going to live a long time. Hospice sent a social worker and nurse to assess Mom for care. As you may know, hospice was formed to help people die with dignity. Nobody thought Mom was dying, so she really didn't qualify for hospice care, but these two young women knew how badly they were needed in the house. I came home and I thought it was going to be fine, but they said there was a problem with qualifying Mom. The three of us went upstairs to the bedroom and they called their supervisor. Mom didn't qualify on paper, but they knew she needed it. They worked with the supervisor who figured out a way to honestly state the case using the information strategically. They did nothing fraudulent but phrased things in a way that made Mom eligible. I was so grateful to those two young women and their supervisor because of that.

That was just before the sheets incident. That afternoon—between when I talked with Dad and when I got home—the hospice nurse was there for a scheduled appointment.

When I arrived home that night the hospice nurse was there and she recommended a respite weekend. Hospice had a section of a nursing home that was for the use of their patients where they could stay to give their caretakers a break. Medicare allowed one respite weekend a year, and it was time for Dad to have his. He was reluctant and worried that no one would take care of her like he did, but the nurse was skilled and respectful, enabling him to take the opportunity.

Margo Arrowsmith

We got her settled in, and although she seemed content, he was worried about the rule that said he could not visit her while she was there. I didn't know what to expect from him. I thought he would be very sad and a little worried, which he was, but he turned to me and said, "Let's go out to dinner."

We went to a diner, and he looked like a kid again. He said, "I haven't been out after dark in fifteen years." It had never occurred to me that something like that would mean so much to him, although I should have thought about it. I knew he was under stress, but he never complained.

Surprisingly, he enjoyed himself. He missed Mom but he enjoyed his weekend. However, when he went to see her on Monday expecting to pick her up, she was happier than she had been in awhile. My mom and dad were one of those couples who never fought; they barely ever disagreed about anything, that he was a Duke fan and she rooted for Carolina was as big as it got. But the last few weeks and months she had been getting kind of crabby with him, nasty even. It was very unlike her to be like that with anyone, and certainly not with Dad.

We talked with the hospice people about it and everyone agreed that she would be better off there. That nursing home was about fifteen minutes from our house, and Dad was still driving. He would get up in the morning without having to worry about taking care of Mom. He took a shower, made breakfast, and would leisurely read his newspaper. Then he would drive to the nursing home and sit at my mother's bedside holding her hand until about a half an hour before dark—he couldn't drive after dark—and then he would drive home. It was working out for her, and it was working out for Dad.

We went to apply for her Medicaid because, again, it was clear their money wasn't going to last that long. Hospice had told us to do this. Dad had to qualify, and it would take a few months. There were two months of Medicare coverage, and then their money had to run out before they qualified for Medicaid. We found out that with an older married couple, they split the money. Her half of it had to be used up, but not his. The helpful woman at Medicaid explained that they did not want the remaining spouse to be destitute, which made a lot of sense. Whatever money they had left, half of it was going to go to Mom's care—and it would have to be spent before Medicaid would take over. The other half was Dad's and wouldn't be touched. She even encouraged him to buy things he needed while she was still covered by Medicare. She was not recommending cheating, but rather helping Dad to make the best decisions.

Dad had macular degeneration by that time and his eyes were getting worse; he did need a different kind of television. He had one of those old-fashioned boxy things that he could barely see; he needed something larger and clearer. He asked the Medicaid representative if that would be acceptable. My dad was not a welfare person; he was certainly not going to cheat the government. She said,

"Of course," so we went shopping and got him a big flat-screen TV that was much easier for him to see. He knew Mom was well taken care of and was happier there. However, he always felt a little guilty about getting a TV, about having a big beautiful TV while she was at her nursing home. He lived with that, but never really got over it.

As I mentioned earlier, Mom had had some surgery to stop large areas from bleeding, but she continued to have small bleeds throughout her body to the point that she was taken to a hospital for a blood transfusion about twice a year. That had worsened even before she went to the nursing home, and it was always a struggle for her to go to the hospital. She was miserable there and she hated it. The doctor came to talk to Dad and said it was time for another one. The time in between was going to get shorter and shorter.

Dad wanted to know what this would be like for Mom. He wanted to know why they couldn't do it at the nursing home, making it easier for her; the more frequent trips to the hospital were the major cause of her distress. Fortunately, she had a doctor who sat with him and explained everything, even when he asked the same questions over and over hoping to get a different answer.

Margo Arrowsmith

Dad would have spent the rest of his life taking care of her, even by himself when he was cleaning up after her and couldn't leave the house. He would have gladly done that. Now that she was in the nursing home and all he had to do was to come and sit, talk with her, and hold her hand, he would have done that for a thousand years. However, the doctor said, "We will keep giving her the transfusions as long as she needs them." Then Dad would ask, "What's it going to be like for her?" and he would answer, "Mr. Arrowsmith, I can tell you that this is very hard on her, and it will get worse." The doctor was very patient with him and answered the same question over and over; when Dad asked the question in a different way, he'd give him a little more information. Finally, Dad looked at him and said, "I can't put her through this." Understand that Dad wanted her to be around forever; he had a great life with her now, but he was not going to put her through something so difficult, and he said

"No." Christmas Eve day, I was doing some errands. Dad was at the nursing home holding Mom's hand. I got a call from the hospice nurse. Mom had passed.

I listen to the debates over the Affordable Care Act, otherwise known as *Obamacare*. People feel a lot of different things about that, but the one thing I want to talk about here is what some call the *death panels*. There began to be a rumor that Obamacare would have death panels that would decide if an elderly person's life was worth the cost of treatment; if they were too old or ill, they wouldn't get care, and that would lead to death. The provision they were referring to gave people the ability to hire a doctor to explain all of the options to them and what each one would mean. The people who were against Obamacare looked at this and made it into something it wasn't. I want to clear this up, because this part of the law is humane and helpful. Dad was lucky that Mom had a doctor who performed the service without extra pay. However, I am concerned that there are people who took that and made it into the opposite of what it really is. Dad felt guilty about buying a TV with Mom in the home, but after that talk—after having all his questions answered, several times, and with his grief and loss of Mom—he never felt guilty about that decision because he knew it had been best for her.

When I got to the nursing home Dad was sitting at her side, still holding her hand. She had been dead about a half an hour. I put my hand on her chest. There is nothing quite as still as a once breathing body that is now without life. Dad and I drove home. We returned once when Dad wanted to take a gift to the nurses to thank them.

We went home that night and watched a tearjerker movie on his new TV. At one point as Dad was sitting in his chair he just shuddered like a boy. I got a sense of the terror he must have felt that moment, knowing he would have to live for however long without my mother. It was another example of how the decision he had made was not for his convenience; it was for her.

The movie was with Sean Penn and Michelle Pfeiffer. Sean Penn played a retarded man whose daughter was being taken away from him by the state. Michelle Pfeiffer was his lawyer. It was a perfect movie to watch as we could both cry, but we were really crying about my mother.

My father had had that time with the doctor when he was able to make an educated decision. While he had felt guilty about buying a TV with Mom in the nursing home, he never once felt guilty for the decision about my mother's transfusions because with the information he had, he knew he had made the best decision for her.

We owe a great debt to both Doctors Making House Calls and to hospice. My mother had a good death, and they helped make it as easy as possible for my dad. However, I can't help but wonder what would have happened–how different it would have been–if we had just gotten some help in there sooner. Maybe things would have been different if my mom had had a home health aide to help Dad with some of the housekeeping and do some of the cleaning up of Mom, or if we'd had somebody to sit with her, so that he could get out and do more things out in the community that he really wanted to do. We can never know for sure, of course. Mom may still have gone to the nursing home, and she probably would have died–but I do know that Dad would have been a whole lot better off, and she may have been able to stay home. She felt better in the nursing home but that was probably because Dad was more relaxed with all that help. If Dad had had the care of the team at home those last couple of months, she might not have been stressed to the point of getting so cranky.

Don't Try This At Home Alone

Yes, teams are very important, and this next section of the L.O.V.E. formula is about organizing a team. I am going to teach you the basics here.

The House

I did parent care in three different housing situations. The first, as I previously mentioned, was in a separate guesthouse/mother-in-law suite in my backyard. There were obvious benefits to this, not the least of which was an enormous amount of privacy and plenty of room.

After Mom died I sold the house, and Dad and I moved into a three-bedroom apartment. This was probably the least ideal situation, but it was manageable. Dad got the bedroom with the en suite bathroom, and I had the two other bedrooms. I used one for an office, and we shared the kitchen. Neither one of us used the living room very much, which was kind of a waste of space and maybe not the best organization, but it worked.

When it came time to buy another house, I made absolutely sure it had a bedroom on the first floor. Dad could still go up and down steps, but it was becoming clear that that was not going to last for very long so we didn't even look at houses that did not have a first floor bedroom. What I ended up getting was ideal: a townhouse with two first floor bedrooms and two upstairs rooms. Dad had the two downstairs bedrooms, and I had the two upstairs. He had one room for sleeping and the other for his living area. We even used the closet and put in a small refrigerator, microwave, and toaster oven · with storage for a few other things he would need. He basically had his own kitchen.

My point is that almost any place can be made to work. The issue is *organization*: how the house is set up and how people learn to respect each other's space and privacy.

There are multiple possibilities for housing. You can care for your parents without them necessarily having to leave their own home, especially if it's close enough to you. If you have a good enough team, your parents could stay in their own home without it being close; that just makes it a little harder for you to manage the team.

The issue is to be creative. You will want privacy for everybody, but you also want to make sure that it's safe and pleasant. Another issue for us — both when looking for the apartment and the house — was that we needed to be on a bus line. If your parents can take a bus, that's even better, but Dad couldn't. We still needed to be on the bus line. Many cities have a transportation program for disabled people. In Dad's case he was legally blind due to the macular degeneration. This meant he could get a cab that would pick him up at the house and take him wherever he wanted to go. It could be the doctor's office or to go bowling — wherever he wanted — and it would pick him up and bring him home. And this all happened for the price of a bus ticket, which was just wonderful. However, it limited me when buying a house or renting an apartment because we had to be on a bus line; that was the other requirement besides having a certified disability.

Building an addition might be one option if you have the finances, but I caution you about this. We assumed that the garage renovation would add to the value of my house and be a great selling point for it. Neither was true; potential buyers didn't know what to do with it and it had cost me time and money. The garage makeover had been perfect for Mom and Dad, but it didn't provide the benefit we assumed. I would have done it anyway, but we should have gotten a professional opinion first.

Margo Arrowsmith

Decide What All of Your Goals Are For an Addition or Conversion

It is important that you make an assessment of what you need after your mom and dad are gone. Do you want the space for a future rental? Do you need that? Is it important that the addition add to the value of the property?

You also need to decide who is going to pay for it. Mom and Dad saved thousands of dollars with their investment in my house, and I lost money. It also caused hard feelings in the family with my brother. While it was still worth doing, it was not a benefit to me, so my paying for the renovations would not have made sense–even if it hadn't been so costly. Just be clear about the upfront expenses and what other issues may come up. It's best to be prepared and not be blindsided. Get it all on paper, and prepare for any irrationality that might come up if the will isn't airtight.

But don't think you have to have something built; if you are creative or find someone who is, you can even make it work in an apartment. Remember the client I had who put up drapes over the dining room arch? That worked for them, and the cost was minimal.

Figure out what you need for you and your family. What are the main issues? Privacy will probably be one of them, but think about what else you use your house for and what you will need to do to keep certain functions. You are not done with the paper, so get it out and put everything down.

Safety is another issue. I had to have at least one downstairs bedroom, but that might not be the case with your parents. If it is an issue and there is no way to make a downstairs bedroom, get a stair elevator; that might be more cost effective than moving. There are many ways to solve problems.

Safety issues of taking care of parents are very similar to those when taking care of children. The place needs to be accident proofed. Install safety bars, grab bars, or handrails around the bath or shower. I installed one on the back deck so that Dad had something to hold onto when coming in from outside. Put sticky tape on the tub floor if you can't do anything else. However, if you do some remodeling, a walk-in shower would be best; one with a seat — or at least a shower chair — is even better. If the money is available, a walk in bathtub is ideal, but they are expensive.

An attachment for the toilet seat to make it higher makes getting up and down safer. They work, but they are unsightly and can be difficult for other people to use. I was also concerned about it being unsanitary. Dad had a new toilet installed that solved the problem for us. It sat higher off the ground, almost as high as a regular toilet with a riser would have been. It looked better, was easier for other people to use, was more sanitary, and it didn't cost all that much. We even had a friend install it for free with some help from me. If you can't get either of those, you can install handrails around the toilet. We did that in addition to the higher seat.

Install at least one stairway handrail, and make sure the stairs are sturdy and clear.

Make sure that stairwells are well lit, and consider making all the lighting in your house brighter. Make sure that rugs — including those on the stairs — are tacked to the floor. Better yet, remove all loose throw rugs leaving none of them on the floor. If you have one that's a family treasure, hang it on the wall; just get it off the floor.

Avoid clutter of any kind. We removed any furniture that was not necessary. All remaining furniture should be stable and without sharp corners to minimize the effects if there is a fall. Dad once fell onto a plastic chair on the deck and it actually broke his fall, although he destroyed the chair — so that was good. But if there is something there, make sure it isn't glass or something that can hurt or cause injury; you want something that isn't going to make it worse if there's an accident.

Change the location of the furniture so that your elderly parent can hold onto something when getting around the house. At some point a walker with wheels is a must in the house as well as outside. My dad was the last person I ever thought would accept one of those, but he did it when he got to the point where he felt he needed it. He got one that had wheels and a seat on it. This was great because if he needed to take something from the kitchen to his room, he could just put it on the seat, so it also worked as a little carrying case. This also works outside if someone is walking and gets tired. If they need to rest they can turn around and sit on it—but Dad would never do that.

Do not have electrical cords trailing across the floor, and be very careful to have additional base plugs installed so that long cords are not necessary. Have your parents wear nonslip shoes or slippers rather than walking around in stocking feet.

Make sure all rooms have adequate lighting, and consider motion-sensitive lights that come on when someone enters the room. Use night lights in every room. Keep frequently used items in cabinets that are easy to reach. Get a grasping tool for reaching. Medicare will pay for the motor for a lifting recliner. You might want to have plastic drinking glasses to use to avoid broken glass when they are home alone.

The Team

The people on your team will vary depending on your parents' needs, their physical and mental condition, and your needs. So, get that paper out again.

Brainstorm this with other people, including your parents. Put everything on this list but don't worry about how to do it right now. Take all suggestions whether you think they are important or not. An example of a need might be based on practicality or modesty. I probably could have gotten Dad in and out of the shower, but it really wasn't something I was trained to do; as his daughter it really wasn't something that I should do.

Add even the mundane things to your list that you probably could do—even simple things like taking them to the grocery store, buying their groceries, and getting them stamps. Add everything you or anyone can possibly think of, even if you feel capable of doing it for them.

Now Make a List of What You Want to Do

What you *can* do for your parents and what you want to do for them may not be the same things at all. Ideally, many of them will be, but there are things you can do that would be burdensome and some things you might want to do but can't—or shouldn't—such as the shower example.

Also know that just because there's something you can or wAlso know that just because there's something you can or want to do now doesn't mean you're going to want to do it—or may even be able to do it—later, so know that this is just a working list; it will change. For example, initially, after Dad stopped driving, I enjoyed taking him to the store. It was a nice outing for us as we each went to get our own things. However, as he got to the point where he walked slower and had a harder time seeing, it became a very slow process to go to the store. It took me much longer. Because of this, I started asking him to make me a list, and I did his shopping for him. Now, if the only thing he needed was getting his stuff from the store, that would have worked out just fine as it didn't take me much longer than doing my own shopping. The problem is that he didn't just need groceries; he needed to get out of the house for exercise and entertainment. My doing it from a list wasn't good for him, but I had neither the time nor the patience to take him anymore. So something I could do turned into something I didn't want to do, and he suffered until we found someone to take him. The independence of getting out of the house and being able to do things—such as doing his own banking—were worth the price of an aide.

At this point we found Queen, who really was a queen in our house. She had all the patience in the world, and we paid her so she didn't mind if it took an hour for Dad to do his grocery shopping. Plus, he didn't just get his groceries; he got the independence of being someone who picked his own groceries out, *and* it got him out of the house for some socialization.

Margo Arrowsmith

What Can Mom or Dad Do?

Caution: Do not do what my grandpa and grandma did.

Orval and Alberta Byrd were a very traditional couple. He had been a railroad telegrapher and station manager for forty-seven years when Grandma had her stroke. He immediately quit his job—he was near retirement anyway–to stay home to take care her. He was used to working hard all day. Grandma was a good mother and an even better grandma, but she was never especially interested in keeping house or cooking. Grandpa, however, had always been a very traditional man who wouldn't do "women's work," but he surprised everyone by taking on the role of househusband with gusto and a vengeance. Even though househusbands weren't very common back in the fifties—and it wasn't even a concept yet—that is exactly what Grandpa was. Grandma, who hated housekeeping and whose children were grown, was very happy to sit in a chair and watch one of the three TV channels that existed. She liked reminiscing about everything from her days of growing up in Arizona to when her kids were in World War II.

Grandpa learned to make noodles from scratch, asked for a vacuum cleaner for Christmas, and was obsessed with the fancy new Melmac (plastic) plates. This was all very amusing and probably very good for him to have that kind of change in his life, but it really wasn't very good for Grandma. As he did more and more for her, she was perfectly content to sit in her chair and do less and less. She became more physically fragile and mentally incapable. My brother and I learned a lot about her constantly retelling old stories, but my cousins avoided her. Mom and Dad said that Grandpa's babying of her actually made her worse; they said they would never do that. I didn't have the heart to remind Dad that he was actually treating Mom the way that Grandpa treated his wife. Parents have to continue to do as much as they can.

Sit down with your parents and figure out what they can still do. If they can't do something, investigate if it's because they're afraid to hurt themselves. If things changed a little bit, would it be okay? For example, Dad was able to go to my kitchen and empty the dishwasher even when his legs were weak because he used his walker. He sat on the walker while he emptied the dishwasher, sometimes leaving the dishes on the counter and sometimes standing and doing it himself. He could also load the dishes that way.

Remember that your parents don't have to do everything. They have earned the right to say they don't want to do some chores, but they also need to be contributing members of the household. That is best for both their physical and mental health.

Get out more paper, and with your parents make a list of what they can do. Then make a list of what they *want* to do and—just as important—what they really *don't* want to do. Make another list about what your parents can do to help you. Be sure to be realistic. Nothing can be gained from showing them that you need things they really can't do, but don't underestimate them either.

So now you should have lists about *cans*, *can'ts*, and *wants*. Determining what these are is part of the process of figuring out who you will need on your initial support team. Dad could do his own shopping, but it wouldn't have been safe for him to take a cab to the store and walk through it alone, and his legal blindness would have made it very hard to find the correct items. However, he *wanted* to go and was capable of doing much of the job himself. I no longer had the patience to take him, but it wasn't very good for him when I did all his shopping. Thus, we knew we needed someone for this job, so that was someone to add to the list of team members we needed.

While I believe that your parents have earned the right to not do some things that they really don't like, I also know it's important to challenge them a little, because that is going to keep them in better shape physically and mentally. Be realistic, and observe.

Margo Arrowsmith

Who Pays?

I suggest you follow Mom's wise words when we started. Don't commingle money. Remember that if it's for their care, their money should go first. I say this because it's only fair. It's *their* care; if they don't spend their money on caring for themselves, it's going to be inherited by you and your siblings. They aren't going to remember how much you spent taking care of them and offer to repay you; at least you can't count on that. To prevent resentment on both sides, just make it clear that Mom and Dad are paying for the caretaking expenses–from buying new furniture to hiring a team. It's just cleaner that way, and those pesky expectations and fantasies will be less likely to cause a family feud after Mom or Dad are gone. Spend the money now, and keep records so that everybody knows where it went. Do not think that after your mom and dad die you'll be able to go to the will reading and say, "It cost me this amount of money for a home health aide, and it cost me this amount of money to make a safe bathroom for them," and that your siblings are going to say, "Okay, let's go ahead and pay for that and add a little for all the work you did." Unless you have a rare family, that just isn't going to happen. In fact, add that to your fantasy list of things you have to let go. Families have broken up at will readings over less than your saying you think you deserve the money you spent on something that involved your parents' care. The whole thing can be solved *now* if you and your parents just agree from the beginning that they will pay for their own expenses — including babysitters and home health aides.

Now, if you really want to use your money, fine, but do it knowing that it is a gift that you shouldn't expect to get back.

List All Current Expenses and Things That May Come Up

Count housing changes as part of those expenses, and things that your mom or dad should pay for. My mom and dad paid for the renovations to turn a 750-square-foot garage into a house; they paid for the additional plumbing and for all of the renovations. Heck, they did a lot of the work. This actually ended up working out just fine for them because after that they paid no rent, and it took about four years for them to break even; then they actually started to make money on that deal. I ended up losing money on it when I went to sell my house. But it would have been much worse if I had also paid for the renovations; I would have lost money. It just made sense for them to do it.

If you want to add a bedroom or bathroom because of what it will do for the value of your house — or if you would have done it anyway — then pay for it yourself, or at least split the cost with your parents. It would be good if your parents could contribute; it's important for their self-respect. Maybe they can at least pay for part of the renovations. For instance, if Mom and Dad want carpeting or a certain kind of floor or bathroom that you might not have chosen, then they could pay for that part of it.

Understand that your siblings may not be able to deal with this, but if your parents are living in your house, then it's between you and your parents, not your siblings. The inheritance will still be partly theirs as long as your parents are there to make decisions for themselves.

When dealing with siblings, explain it to them once and only once, as constant repeating of the same discussion isn't going to change their thinking; it will just wear you down. Answer new questions, and give appropriate information and facts, but only if Mom or Dad want to. In fact, let *them* do it if they can. But don't have the same conversation over and over to no conclusion.

Regardless of who pays — but especially if you do — check with a real estate expert to make sure that renovating is going to be financially viable for you. In my situation it wasn't financially viable at all; however, it was something I wanted to do, and I still would have done it. But if it's important to you to either not lose money or to even make money on it, check with a real estate agent first. If you don't like what you hear, then think of an appropriate alternative.

Margo Arrowsmith

When Mom and Dad lived in the guest house we had one electrical system throughout the entire house. They heated with electricity and I heated with gas. Mom suggested at the beginning that since there were two of them and one of me that they would pay two-thirds of the bill. Even though I heated their house, they basically paid two thirds of the electric bill. It didn't quite work out, but I agreed to that, and it was fine. Your situation will be different, and of course there are many possibilities. Just make sure that everyone is clear on the plan when they move in.

When Mom died, Dad lost her Social Security, which was basically a little less than half of his income; I think it scared him. He wasn't comfortable talking to me about it so he just stopped paying his part of the electricity. While I advise differently, I didn't say anything. In your situation, however, you might want to be clear about this. If it had been a great hardship for me, I might have said something to him, but I didn't want to make him uncomfortable.

Having learned a lot during the experience, I would have done it differently.

Dad paid for his own food, his own transportation, and his own medical expenses. That included the home health aides when we needed them until he died. Sometimes that was a bit of a problem because he didn't want to spend the money to get as much help as he needed. But by the end he knew he really needed the help, and it worked out.

Have your parents pay for as much as possible, but if you want to pay for expenses make sure of two things. First, make sure you can easily afford it and that it won't take away from your retirement or your children's education. Second, don't expect to get any money back at the time of the will reading. Don't expect them to put something in the will that says that you will be paid back for all your sacrifices; that's not going to happen. Make it clear to your siblings what the plan is at the time care starts–or better yet have your mom or dad do it. Or, just realize that it really isn't your siblings' business. Its your parents' money, it isn't your siblings' money.

Understand that your parents may not want to discuss this with your siblings or leave them less. They love your siblings, even more than you do, and they aren't going to want to hurt them. Besides, remember that you can't expect that what you think is fair or your due is going to happen.

Life Insurance

When my parents came to live with me I was long past having dependents and hadn't had life insurance in many years. However, as Mom wisely pointed out, if I died for any reason they would still need a place to live. There was no way they were going to be able to afford the mortgage on my house. I got a life insurance policy that was big enough to cover the mortgage. I recommend that, but do not make your parents the beneficiaries unless you want the money to go to your siblings after your parents die. In my case, I made my daughter the beneficiary with the stipulation that it be used for the mortgage. The will read that the house was hers, but she could not sell it as long as my parents needed to live there. Had I done it differently and my parents had outlived me, the money would have to be shared with my sibling and his children. I love my nieces, but I did not work to leave them money in place of my daughter.

You may love your nieces and nephews, but most likely you want your money to go to your children. That won't happen unless you make careful plans to both care for your parents in your absence *and* protect your children.

When Dad and I lived in the apartment, I made my grandchildren the beneficiaries of the life insurance policy. I didn't have a mortgage then, but I knew that without me Dad would need more money for care and a place to live, so I kept the term policy. I knew I could trust my daughter to understand that until Dad died, the money from the policy was for his housing and care. I put her in charge of it until Dad died, at which point whatever money hadn't been spent to care for Dad would go to her children. Again, if I had just made him the beneficiary of the policy, when he died that money would have gone to my brother, not my children. That would have put Dad in a position of leaving his son out, and he couldn't do that. If you have any concerns, talk to an attorney or at least an insurance agent in your state.

At my age, a term life insurance policy—which is all I recommend you get—was over a hundred dollars a month. I canceled it as soon as he died. It was well worth knowing that he would have had what he needed for his living expenses and care if I had preceded him in death.

The Team

Professionals

Make a List of All Doctors

This means *every* doctor. Dad had had cancer twenty years earlier and still had a check-up every five years. I put that doctor on the list; every doctor with any connection at all goes on this list. Your parents must be part of this process. Do it as a brainstorming session.

Include your parents as part of the process, and engage them in a discussion about their experiences with these doctors. You know your parents. If they are hesitant to talk about a particular doctor, it might be time to probe some more. For example, some of the questions you should ask are: are they seen promptly at appointments or do they usually have to wait? If so, for how long? Do they expect to have to wait in the waiting room for two, three, or four hours? Do they leave your parents sitting in the examining room for a long time before the doctor comes in? Is the staff friendly? Are appointments made with your parents' needs in mind? All of this matters.

You also want to know if these doctors know of each other. In a big city it's unlikely that all of them—or even *any* of them—know each other. But do they have a way of communicating with each other? If you have the time, it would be nice for you to visit as many of these doctors as you can with your parent.

Dad had been going on his own doctors' appointments for a long time before I started caring for him. I had taken him to his macular degeneration doctor because he couldn't drive after the treatment of shots to his eyes, so I knew them personally. I knew that they were efficient and friendly and that Dad's appointments were on time. But I had to rely on information from him about the other doctors. Of course, it was not for me to make him change a doctor, but it helped to know who they were.

If you can attend any appointment, there are important issues to be aware of. Does the doctor look your parent in the eye when answering a question? When your parent asks a question, does the doctor answer him or her, or does the doctor look to you? It's possible that in this case the doctor is trying to make a connection with you, but it's also possible that this is a sign of disrespect. This can be a clue as to what this doctor thinks about the capability of your parent or old people in general. If this happens in an appointment, ask Mom or Dad what it feels like for them. You want to get a sense of how well the doctors listen to your parents, how well they communicate with your parents, and, frankly, how respectful they and their staff are of elderly people.

An essential book for anyone who sees doctors (in other words, *everyone*) is How Doctors Think by Jerome Groopman. I highly recommend it. It's very readable but has essential information that could save lives. It's written by a doctor who discusses how doctors are trained and how that can affect patient care negatively. He gives a straightforward method of how to ask questions in a way that will help the doctor break out of his or her training to give a better diagnosis and better care to your parents—and to you for that matter.

I recommend hiring a professional nurse as a consultant. I'm suggesting a nurse because they are more affordable than doctors but they can be just as knowledgeable. Your doctor is a consultant but you need an *advocate*. You need someone who can help explain what's going on and what all the possibilities are.

Margo Arrowsmith

I talked about the day Mom called in a panic when Dad was in a fetal position on the living room floor. As I stated, the EMS came and took him to the hospital, and I had to stay with my mom because she could not be left alone. I had assumed it would be just like every other time he'd gone to the hospital. I planned go get him the next day or the day after and that all would be well. I got a call from the hospitalist the next day, a Sunday, saying Dad was ready to come home. I had no reason to believe that my dad was *not* ready to come home. In fact, I expected to get there and be back home in that magic half hour that Mom could be left alone.

When I got to the hospital and rounded the corner, the first thing I saw was the nurses' station. I was looking for Dad's room when I saw a man in a hospital gown tied to a chair waving his arms around talking crazily; he seemed to be floridly hallucinating. It was my father, right in front of the nurses' station. My initial response was horror and pain upon seeing my father in those humiliating circumstances; that was immediately followed by panic. I couldn't take him home like that; what would I do with him?

First things first. I had to figure out how we were going to get through the day. What could I do to advocate for my father and myself? What did I need to know? Fortunately, I had professional experience with mental health; I knew symptoms and some of the lingo. But I needed help.

I called my friend Lisa who went to take care of my mom. It was the first time I had reached out for help. Fortunately, it was Sunday so she wasn't at work. I settled in to take care of him because there was no way they could untie him unless I was there to provide constant supervision. I understood they didn't have a nurse who could be with him all day. So I sat with him in his room and did reality orientation. I took him for walks. When he decided he wanted to walk I got up and followed him to keep him from getting into any trouble.

The hospitalist kept coming in to tell me to take him home. He tried to manipulate me into taking him home by saying, "They get confused when in strange places, and he will be better off at home because being in the hospital is damaging his fragile sense of reality." My professional experience told me that this wasn't confusion; it was *hallucinations* — two very different things. I explained that to the doctor. I also said that between my parents, Dad had been here a lot in the last year, so it wasn't a strange place. It probably didn't help much, but I added, "Frankly, when he's not having pneumonia and hallucinating because of the pneumonia, he's a lot smarter than you are." I was not at my professional best, but this was personal. This man was going to harm my father by sending him home when he wasn't ready.

This was a constant battle. Every few minutes the doctor would come in to pressure me. I was shocked that he had so much time. I called my brother in California. His wife had been a longtime nurse and most recently was the head of the utilization review department in a hospital; she was one tough cookie. I put her on the phone the next time the doctor came in. He lost all color in his face at the end of the conversation and said that my father would be staying in the hospital.

I left when Dad was tired enough to sleep, and I knew that he wouldn't be tied up any more. The next day the hallucinations were basically gone so we didn't have to worry about that again.

I knew that this business about being confused in a strange place was the doctor trying to manipulate me. I knew they were trying to get me to take Dad home because on a Sunday they couldn't get authorization to leave him there. They were worried they might not get paid. I was armed with the knowledge of how the system works. I also had years of professional experience with manipulators; it was my job to spot manipulators. This doctor was a professional manipulator. I had experience and information that most people don't have.

After we got it settled that Dad was going to stay and that he didn't need to be tied up, I went home, exhausted. I woke up in the middle of the night and thought, *What if the doctor was right? What if I did Dad an injustice by leaving him there?* Then I thought, *My God, if this guy got me doubting myself, what would it be like for people with no background in these issues? What would it be like for someone who didn't have my sister-in-law as a backup?*

Margo Arrowsmith

I was correct. Dad ended up staying another five days in the hospital, longer than he had stayed when he had had his heart surgery and another week in rehab. If that doctor could get me to second-guess myself like that, what would someone do who had no background in any of this? I had my sister-in-law to step in and you may need the cavalry reinforcement also.

I thought I could handle being there by myself all day, but I was so grateful when I saw my friend, Ellen, walking down the hall to keep me company. Lisa had called her and they didn't think I should be alone all day. I repeat, don't try this alone. Thanks to both of them, and my sister -in-law I didn't have to that day.

This is why I think it's so important to have someone who you know understands medical issues, financial issues, and how to talk to doctors. It's so important to have somebody who can explain things to you, who can advocate for you and your parent. If I had a client in the hospital who called me and told me the circumstances, I would explain to them why the doctor was manipulating them into taking the father home. I would explain the difference between confusion and hallucinations–in this case, hallucinations that were caused by severe fever from pneumonia. But I also could have used someone who was more of a purely medical person, a nurse or nurse practitioner.

I recommend doing some research to find someone. Advertise on Craigslist, go to a nursing school, go to a hospital, or go to a nursing staffing agency. Ask for someone who can spend maybe an hour a month going over your parents' medical issues and medications, explaining them to you and looking for any cross problems that might not have been noted by one of many specialists. Also ask for someone who can give you information and support in a crisis.

I don't think this is an actual profession, but you may be able to find someone. It *should* be a recognized profession.

List All Meds

I once called a nursing hotline at Blue Cross Blue Shield. I had Blue Cross Blue Shield insurance myself at the time so my question had to do with me, but I mentioned to the nurse that my dad was on a lot of medications. He was on three or four different blood pressure medications that had been given to him by an assortment of doctors, some of whom he no longer saw, but new doctors just renewed them. It drove me crazy. Her statement was very challenging, but intriguing. She said, "Go to the doctors, and tell them to pick two or three medications. He will take those and no more." Her theory was that doctors keep prescribing medications because that's all they know how to do—because they *can* and because people will take whatever they are told to take by doctors. If a doctor had to pick only three medications, he or she would quickly narrow it down for the betterment of the patient. I once told that to a doctor, and he said he doubted that she ever really said that. She may have been incorrect, but she said it. I am not advocating that any of you do this. It is something to think about. Many people—and certainly most elderly people—are on way too much medication. I recently had to go to the ER and ended up in emergency surgery. They couldn't believe that I was sixty-five years old and on no medication at all. Elderly people tend to have several doctors because they have different ailments; each doctor often acts without discussing it with the patient's other doctors.

> ## *What to Ask About All Current Medications and Added Medications*
>
> 1. What is the purpose of this medication?
>
> 2. How does it do its job?
>
> 3. Is it doing its job?
>
> 4. What are the side effects?
>
> 5. Are other medications being prescribed to handle the side effects?
>
> 6. How does this medication react with every other medication?
>
> 7. What would happen without the medication?

Medications

The first thing you need to do is write down all medications that your parents are taking. That includes over-the-counter medication; it includes everything. As you write them down, look at the bottle to see the dosage and the name of the doctor. You can look up medications on the Internet to see what they are supposed to do.

Your next step should be to have someone look at them and see if there are problems with drug interactions. Your pharmacy may advertise that they do that automatically. I've seen the ads, but these pharmacies have thousands of customers, and they can't logistically do that for everyone. You will have to advocate there, but it will be worth it.

You can go to the pharmacy to ask for a meeting with the pharmacist. Pharmacists go to college for five years to do what they do. They probably enjoy being able to actually put some of that training into practice. Some will welcome your request. However, they don't have a lot of time. It's likely that they are working for a big corporation that has other claims on their time. They also can't ruffle too many feathers, as the corporations make money when drugs are sold. A pharmacist may not be able to be as candid as you would like.

Dad was hallucinating in the hospital, but it wasn't a mental disorder; it was due to his fever. A year later as we drove down Capital Boulevard in Raleigh, Dad giggled and said, "Well if I was in Winslow, Arizona I would believe my eyes, but here we are in Raleigh, North Carolina and I'm seeing an Indian man walk down the street with a blanket on and feathers in his hair. I don't think it's here." I shared the joke and told him that no, there was no Indian. Dad's eyes were fooling him, but his brain was working, and he knew that that wasn't logical. I said, "Dad, the last time you hallucinated was because you had pneumonia." I suggested taking him to the ER so this could be dealt with before he got that sick again. He wasn't happy about it, but agreed when I pulled out my trump card: *Who will take care of Mom if you get really sick?* I wasn't above manipulation myself. I dropped him off at the hospital and went home to be with Mom.

I returned to the ER later to get him, and the doctor confirmed that he did have some pneumonia; they had given him antibiotics. They wanted to keep him overnight. Neither of us wanted that, but we conceded while asking for a promise that he would not see a hospitalist. That promise was not kept.

Margo Arrowsmith

I went to pick him up the next day; he was more than ready to go. They explained to me that they wanted to keep him for one more night. They had put him on a new medication and wanted to monitor his reaction. I asked what it was and was told *Zyprexa*.

I swear that while we were there on the fifth floor people on the first floor thought there was an earthquake. Well, maybe not that, but they had put Dad on an anti-psychotic medication that has common usage for schizophrenia. This is a serious psychotic condition that strikes between the ages of fifteen and twenty-five. My eighty-eight year old father was not schizophrenic. I went with the nurse to look it up and discovered that it caused more problems with blood pressure, which was why they had added more blood pressure medication.

If I had not been in mental health and specifically worked with psychotics, I would not have known what this medication was.

I asked a psychiatrist friend of mine about Zyprexa—how did it work? It works by dulling the brain so that the paranoia and hallucinations are not as strong. My father was nearing ninety, and he had had two bouts of hallucinations in his late eighties, both due to a high fever. To treat that, they gave him an anti-psychotic drug that is designed to dull the brain, the last thing an elderly person needed. If I had not known what that drug was, Dad would have stayed on it and suffered the side effects for nothing.

The nurse didn't want to discuss this at the station any more as there were other people there. I suggested that perhaps these people needed to know what to look out for. I took Dad home. We were forced to sign out against medical advice or AMA even though the pneumonia had been treated, because they wanted him on antipsychotics.

A few years later as I was talking to the mother of one of my clients who is schizophrenic and taking Zyprexa, I started to tell this story. She worked as a clerk in a pharmacy in a big chain store. Before I got to the part about Zyprexa, she said, "I know what they gave him— they gave him Zyprexa, right?" She said that she noticed a lot of old people coming in with that prescription. She went on to say that she had discussed it with the pharmacist who had just shrugged. This woman risked her job for others because when some elderly person came in with this prescription, she asked them if they knew what it was. They never did know what it was or why they were given it, but they filled it anyway.

Hearing that, I went home, and I searched *Zyprexa* and *old people*. I found a couple of disturbing articles. This is a medication that is catching on with doctors; a lot of them are prescribing it to old people. Pharmaceutical companies spend billions of dollars a year to wine and dine doctors to teach them that getting drugs to people is a good thing. However, what I found on the Internet is that the drug company that makes Zyprexa is advising doctors against this practice to no avail. I went to my own pharmacy and asked the clerk about this. She had noticed an increase in this prescription with old people.

This story is important to understand why you may want an independent advocate who can explain medications to you. Obviously, not all doctors prescribe like this—and not all pharmacists would shrug—but it behooves you to have your own person for an hour a month. Add knowledge of pharmacology to your list of requirements when looking for this advocate.

Get somebody to advise you on this—someone you can trust who will look out for you.

Home Health Aides

Yes, home health aides cost some money, but ultimately they will save you a fortune in assisted living or nursing home costs. If your parent meets the medical necessity, as my dad and mom did, Medicare will pay for certain services, but even if it is all private pay, it's worth it.

Margo Arrowsmith

Where I live, home health aides cost an average of twenty five dollars an hour if you get them from an agency. Medicaid will pay for this if your parent qualifies. Medicare will pay for limited use, but you must speak with them about your specific issues. And in either event, home health care has to be prescribed by a doctor, unless it is private pay.

Home health aides will do some light housekeeping, prepare some meals, and some of them will take your parent shopping or out for appointments. Most of them probably can't use their own car; you have to check with the agency's policies on that one. And if you request something that is *not* covered you will have to pay for it. Medicare and Medicaid don't pay for shopping trips. If the aides use their cars, remember that they don't get paid much. They don't get paid twenty five dollars an hour; they get paid about eight to ten dollars an hour, and they've probably had to travel a couple times a day to get to different jobs. If you want them to take your parent to the store or do anything else, you should chip in for gas and wear and tear on their cars.

They can also play cards with your parent or do other things, although technically that's not allowed. However, most of them spend three hours at a clip. There usually isn't that much housekeeping or other things that need doing, so it's nice to have other things that they can do with your mom or dad, as long as the necessary work is done.

You can hire an aide from an agency or you can go private. The benefits of an agency are that the agency has screened these home health aides ahead of time; they have done a criminal check and followed references. They also have several people on staff, so that if one doesn't work out there is another one — as long as you are realistic. Additionally, if your aide is sick or on vacation the agency should have a replacement. The agency also takes care of liability insurance if an aide is injured in your home, IRS issues and other details that can be time consuming and expensive.

The benefits of hiring one on your own are that you can pay them more while costing you less. If an agency charges twenty dollars — and again that varies from state to state and town to town — but they only pay the aide $8.00, there is a twelve dollar difference which the agency uses to pay their overhead and make some profit. There is nothing wrong with that; they earn their money, and this is a taxing business. But if you hire someone *yourself* there is the twelve dollar difference. You can split the difference and pay fourteen dollars an hour. The aide would make six dollars an hour more and you would pay six dollars less. You can advertise on places like Craigslist or nursing schools that you are paying more. You should have the cream of the crop doing that. However, there will still be highly qualified aides who prefer the safety of an agency over making more money. But if you get someone and pay more, they may be more loyal to you and your parent. Don't forget to do criminal checks and reference checks. You will also want to have some backups. You will have to provide all the tax forms at the end of the year. There are people who prefer the private method, but if you choose to do this on your own you will begin to understand why the agencies earn their money. Being an aide or managing aides is hard work. Do not begrudge any of them their money.

There are people who do both. They hire an agency to take care of the Medicare/Medicaid services and then hire other people privately who do other services such as shopping trips. This is not as complicated as it sounds.

Know that there are good agencies, mediocre agencies, and bad agencies. If you are not happy, first talk with the administration. If the issue doesn't get resolved, then go to another agency. There are lots of them out there; they have a lot of competition.

When Dad needed help, I asked around at work to find someone privately. We found a lovely woman, a very good cook who stayed the usual three hours and did some housekeeping. She cooked Dad a great breakfast and lunch, but there was really nothing else for her to do. She was nice, and Dad was sociable, but he wasn't comfortable having someone in the house that long, and she didn't know what else to do. Additionally, she really wanted to do a day care center for children.

Margo Arrowsmith

We could have saved some time if we had gone to an agency in the first place. What I ended up doing was hiring an agency worker who was sent to the house to give showers and for other work, *with the permission of the agency.*

About this time it was getting dangerous for Dad to get in and out of the shower. The only showers we had downstairs were a shower within a bathtub, so he had to step up. It was dangerous, and cleanliness was very important to Dad so he was unhappy. This was the one thing that could have put him in a home. I wasn't trained to give showers, and it is a special skill; plus, neither of us would have been comfortable taking the father/daughter relationship into the shower.

The weekly RN he had at the time (referred by the angels at Doctors Making House Calls) arranged for someone to come three times a week to give Dad a shower. When I first heard about this I thought that he would never put up with it, but boy was I wrong. He loved it and he loved her.

The aide was named Queen and it was a perfect name for her as she was quite a presence. She was a lovely woman with a lot of personality and enthusiasm. She did good work, and he loved her; she loved him in return. It was clear that the problem with the other aide was that three-hour stretch. I approached Queen and asked her if she would be interested in doing things for Dad in shorter spurts of time. Since she was used to being at people's houses for a half an hour, she was used to doing more travel.

She got permission to spend her off hours with Dad. She came before work and made his breakfast, returned during her lunch hour, and then after work she would take him to the store. She could also arrange her schedule for other trips such as doctor visits. This was perfect for us.

Queen was a nurse, so got paid more, but she was the one who could split hours. She wasn't a very good cook, but on our list of priorities, the split shifts were more important. Medicare continued to pay for three showers a week, but Dad wanted one more so we paid for that at a higher, more skilled rate. The whole thing had to be documented very carefully so as to not commit fraud, but Queen took care of that.

She also became an important part of Dad's social schedule, something he looked forward to every day. The important point here is to understand your needs and to be creative. There was also some luck involved in our case, so keep your eye out for opportunities.

You must figure out exactly what you want and what you need. Get out the paper again, and make the list. Do this whether you plan on using an agency, going private, or doing a combination. Make a wish list. You may not get everything you want on that wish list but make the list anyway. When you go to interview an agency or an individual, talk to them about what you want. You might even find an agency that is able to break up the visits, sending someone a little while in the morning and a little while in the afternoon instead of being there for three consecutive hours. I go into a lot of people's houses where they have home health aides; they will tell you that the three hours really doesn't work very well for anybody. There are a lot of times when I get to someone's home and the home health aide is sitting and watching TV. It's not their fault; it's just that there isn't always three hours of things to do. A wish list will help you decide what will work best for you, your family, and your parent. Knowing exactly what you want isn't a guarantee you will get it, but you can bet you *won't* get it if you don't articulate exactly what you want.

Remember That This Is Both an Intimate and a Professional Relationship

Be clear that initially you have to keep the relationship with the aide very professional. Having an aide come into your home is a very intimate thing. It's intimate for them, and it's intimate for your parents. That can be a lovely thing, but you have to be careful because feelings can get hurt very easily. Sometimes the client expects too much personal interaction, and sometimes the aide does. You just have to be careful. The key is to start out from the beginning being very professional; then see what happens and how it's going to work.

Talk to your mom or dad about what goes on during the day. If the aide is supposed to do light housekeeping and you come home to a mess, you can observe that. Do remember that light housekeeping is just that. It isn't spring cleaning, and they aren't there to clean up after the dog or to clean your rooms. If your mom or dad appears to be really hungry, then she or he is not being fed properly. Ask what is happening. Is the person spending more time watching TV or working? TV can be tricky. Watching TV together can be a social activity but it can also be isolating. Are they watching your parent's show or the aide's show, for example?

If your parent isn't a good reporter or is one of those people who never wants to say anything bad, you might even want to consider a nanny cam. I am going to advise you that you should not get too excited about everything you see on the nanny cam. Don't expect that this person being paid eight dollars an hour will do more than they have to. The nanny cam is more to make sure that they aren't being rude, abusive, or ignoring your parent.

Explain to the aide how your parent wants to be addressed. Are first names okay or do they want Mr. or Mrs.? My dad had an RN, Tara, whom he loved — and she loved him. Her job was to do vitals, to check his meds, and do all of that kind of thing, but she was friendly and she clearly cared about him. She always called him Mr. Arrowsmith, but Dad wanted her to call him Fritz. All my life young people called him Fritz, including my parents' friends' children. She nicely explained that because she had grown up in Alabama where all adults were Mr. or Mrs., she just couldn't. She didn't address older people by their first name, and she just couldn't get herself to do it here. She said she also didn't think it was very professional. Had it been the other way around — if she had come in calling him Fritz without asking, or if he had been uncomfortable about being called that — it would have been a whole other situation. But she was being respectful. If your parent is more formal, be sure that all the workers at the agency know that your parent wants to be called Mr. or Mrs.

About the time that we hired Queen to come in three times a day, Dad was doing better. Medicare had decided that since they were paying her to be there, his needs were covered—especially since she could also do the medication. Tara's last day was a tearful one. We all smiled when Dad asked, "Can you call me Fritz now"? She still couldn't, though.

Respect for your parents is as important as the care, sometimes more so. I actually threw a woman out of my house for the way she was treating Dad. Before we found Queen, I had come home when a new aide was there. I was out in the kitchen and could hear them talking. It sounded like everything was going fine, so I just thought I'd go in and sit in his room to see what was going on. I only listened to the conversation they were having, and since Dad was doing fine I certainly didn't want to interrupt. After I got in there, it changed. Dad asked her a question, and she'd look at me and answer. I was sitting on the other side of the room; it's not like we were sitting next to each. After this happened a couple of times I said, "I would appreciate that when Dad asks a question you answer *him*, not me." But she continued; I became more stern and changed it from a request to an order. It continued, so I finally stepped in telling her that if she didn't stop she would have to leave. She continued, and I ordered her out.

She looked shocked, but finally left. I was a little afraid that Dad would be upset that I had made a fuss, but he looked at me and thanked me because he hadn't liked that either. He was aware of what she was doing, and he didn't like it anymore than I did; he just couldn't speak up for himself. Respect is one of the most important aspects of care.

You know your parents. Some parents complain about everything. If your parents are in that category you have to take the complaints with a grain of salt without totally ignoring them. However, if you replace an aide based on your parents' complaints and they *continue* to complain, at some point you have to understand what is happening.

Also, remember that there might be things that you don't like about somebody but your mom or dad may *love* her. If Dad liked the woman mentioned above and didn't care about what she was doing, I probably wouldn't have said anything. I based my guess on sixty years of knowing him. But ultimately, unless there is gross incompetence, the call isn't yours—it is your parent's.

Be careful not to be overly friendly in the beginning. I have seen cases where a lonely patient took the friendliness of a home health aide to heart and started to believe that they were friends who would go out together. Your aide may love your parent very much, but that doesn't mean that it isn't still a job. If that isn't handled properly, hurt feelings can ruin a good working relationship. Conversely, I've seen aides who expect too much; they think it's okay to come in late every day, and that can become a problem. *Friendly* does not mean that you're not working hard or borrowing money—or anything that one might do with a real friend. Just keep your eye out for that.

By the way, I think children can be a bit of a different thing. If your aide's child is home for teacher workday, for example—and if it's okay with your parents—I don't have a problem with bringing the child to the home as long as the child is well behaved. It makes things easier for the worker, your parent won't have an interruption in service, and you can win the heart and loyalty of an aide. And of course, having well-behaved kids around can be good for your parents. Just be careful—it's got to be a *well-behaved* child, and it can't happen on a regular basis.

Again, know that it's very important that your parent agrees with this. You may think it's good for them to have a kid around but they may not.

Ten Things to Look at When Hiring a Home Health Aide

1. The agency should be licensed by the state.

2. The agency should have at least one million dollars in liability coverage.

3. The agency must do criminal background checks on all employees.

4. There should be at least two references check for all staff.

5. The agency should have an on-call person for any concerns a client might have.

6. The agency should have an RN who fulfills the role of clinical director. She should be able to provide a plan of care for any changes in health or needs of the client, and she shold visit the home every ninety days.

7. The agency should make an attempt to match not only the skill set of the staff member but also personalities.

8. Billing issues should be addressed at the outset of the relationship. This includes the frequency of bills, required deposits, and other issues.

9. The agency should have good customer service with someone to listen to your concerns. THen yu should call the state complaints hotline to see how many complaints have been filed against the agency and the nature of those complaints. Remember that not all complaints are valid so everyone will probably have some.

10. The staff should be employees and not independent contractors so that the agency whold be liable and legally accountabl for its actions

Eight Essential Dos and Don'ts for In-house Staff Etiquette

1. Always be friendly while maintaining the boundaries that are needed in a professional relationship.

2. Have a plan of care that clarifies youir expectations; give the aide a clear ideaof what she needs to do to comply.

3. Always have cash, valuables, and important papers locked in a secure location so there is never an opportunity to suspect staff of stealing. Staff usually appreciates this also.

4. Indicate which restrooms in your home you want the staff to use. This should be a powder room, if available.

5. Indicate where you would like staff to park.

6. If staff will be transporting your parent, have copies of the aide's insurance, registration, and driver's license and make sure the aide's documents are in good standing. It is appropriate to check his or her driving record. Pay for gas and wear and tear on the car. Establish this reimbursement before the first outing.

7. If the shift is longer than four hours, there should be a ten-minute break. If it is eight hours, there should be a thirty-minutes break with no expectations of work during that time.

8. Express what is acceptable for cell phone usage adn texting. No more than two short personal calls per shift is common, but only if necessary.

What Medicare Will Do

When I heard that Dad was going to get a woman to bathe him I thought he would never allow it. I was wrong. I also assumed incorrectly that Medicare did not do in-home care. They are very specific about what they will do, but they will pay for some care that is prescribed by a doctor.

Here are the rules and limitations: Medicare doesn't pay for twenty-four hour a day care, meals delivered to the home, homemaker services, or personal care. I would put bathing under personal care but apparently they don't. It never hurts to ask; as I said, I would have assumed that bathing was personal care. They classify things under their own regulations.

Who Is Eligible?

All people with Medicare who meet all of these conditions are covered.

1. A person must be under the care of a doctor and getting services under a plan of care established and regulated by a doctor.

2. A doctor must carefully certify that you need one or more of the intermittent skilled nursing care procedures other than just drawing blood.

3. Physical therapy, speech language pathology, or continued occupational services are covered only when services are specific to the safe and effective treatment of your condition. The amount, frequency, and time period of the services need to be reasonable. They need to be complex and something only a qualified therapist can do safely and effectively.

4. To be eligible, either (1) your condition must be expected to improve in a reasonable and generally predicted time period, or (2) you need a skilled therapist to develop a safe and effective maintenance program for your condition.

5. The home health agency providing care must be certified by Medicare.

6. The patient must be homebound, and a doctor must certify that he or she is homebound. (Dad wasn't totally homebound so this can be resolved in some cases.)

7. A patient is not eligible for home health benefits if he or she needs more than intermittent part-time skilled nursing care.

8. If you need to leave home for medical treatment or short infrequent excursions for non-medical reasons (such as attending religious services) you may still qualify if you need daily adult care.

9. Equipment can be included in payment, such as a motorized wheel chair or the motor for a lift chair.

Call Medicare for clarification on any of these rules. Remember that their rules change. You can get an appointment or get information on the phone. Your doctor's office may also have someone who negotiates with Medicare.

Finding Volunteers or Near Volunteers Organizations

Your community is filled with organizations that serve.

Make a list of organizations that your parents belong to, such as Lions Club, Rotary International, sororities, fraternities, and churches. Put everything on the list.

These organizations usually have some volunteer requirements for their members to do. Sometimes members do individual work, and sometimes work is done in groups. You can get individuals to come to play cards for socialization or build ramps for wheelchairs. They may have group activities that your parents can attend.

The best would be if your parent is a member of a group that will allow him or her to volunteer to help others.

The Boy Scouts and other youth groups are also a source of volunteers. That old saying about the Boy Scout helping the little old lady across the street does not preclude one taking her for the whole walk. In my area most of the high schools—both private and public— have a volunteer requirement for graduation. Every student must have done something for somebody else in order to be able to graduate.

Make a list of all of the possibilities and a list of what you're looking for to pair your parent's needs with what an organization offers. Be open. An organization may have a volunteer service that you could use but haven't thought about.

Neighbors

There are women in your neighborhood who are already geared for caretaking; these are called stay-at-home moms. These are women who might be open to having a little bit of extra money for working just a couple of hours a day. If their kids are at school, they may have time in the morning to take your mom or dad for a trip to the store or the doctor. If she has babies a great idea would be to put the little one in a car seat with mom or dad in the front while going to the store or the park for a little picnic. She would be happy to earn a little extra money while being home for her kids; your mom or dad get the grocery shopping done and you don't have to do it. Your parent may enjoy time with a baby, which could be a bonus. All of that could be worth a little extra money when you think of all the possibilities of everything that could get done.

Think about some of the neighborhood kids who can come over to play cards or read out loud for a blind parent. Perhaps they could help your mom or dad do their chores safely. Open your imagination.

As I said earlier, most of the home health agencies work in shifts of three or four hours; that might be a bit much for your parent to have someone around that long, and it's hard to fill that much time. However, the stay-at-home mom next door may be happy to come over five times a week and make lunch and do a little chatting with your parents. An agency can't send an aide for an hour a day, but you might get a neighbor who is willing to do it for an extra ten dollars or so. Be creative about this. It could cost you very little to have your parent become more connected to the neighborhood — and you will have less to do when you get home.

Churches

Many churches have something called a Stephen's Ministry. Church members are trained as peer counselors. They usually get some supervision from a professional after the training. They are taught to deal with minor and I do mean minor depression or some kind of loss issues, but some of them are just nice to have around for talking; a new face in the house. Your parents might get tired of seeing just you.

Call the minister and ask him or her if there is somebody who can take your mom or dad to the Wednesday night potluck, or some other activity. This might not be something you want to go to, but if someone can give your mom or dad a ride, then it's worth a call. The worst thing that can happen is that they won't have anyone to do it; just ask.

Use the following pages to do the exercises to decide what your team will be. These will be done with your parents, siblings and maybe others.

Margo Arrowsmith

You Can Keep Your Parents At Home

Margo Arrowsmith

You Can Keep Your Parents At Home

Margo Arrowsmith

You Can Keep Your Parents At Home

You Can Keep Your Parents At Home

Margo Arrowsmith

You Can Keep Your Parents At Home

Margo Arrowsmith

One person caring about another represents life's greatest value.

—Jim Rohn

I've learned that regardless of your relationship with your parents, you'll miss them when they're gone from your life.

—Maya Angelou

Life's challenges are not supposed to paralyze you; they're supposed to help you discover who you are.

—Bernice Johnson Reagon

Even at the end Dad let Zoe and Leo in and out, it was appreciated and he contributed.

Chapter 8

Value

Martin Seligman wrote a groundbreaking book about depression, *Learned Depression*. His theory was that depression was learned helplessness. People who think they can't do anything to change their lives or affect their lives get depressed.

They did experiments with dogs to test this out, since they couldn't ethically get people depressed on purpose. Dogs are remarkably similar in personality to human beings; perhaps that's why we love them so. He took dogs and put them through a maze. Every time they completed the maze there would be some kind of reward; of course the dogs were very happy to do this.

They started playing around with the dogs—sometimes the food would be there and sometimes it wouldn't. The dog could never count on the food being there. The theory was that the dogs had no way of feeling that they had any part in whether the food was going to be there or not. It didn't matter how good of a job they did; if the food wasn't there, it wasn't there. The dogs had no control over it. The dogs would get very depressed, just as predicted. Then they wondered if giving the dogs more control would alleviate their depression. They found that this was not quite as easy as the first step. They started putting food at the end of the maze every time, but they just couldn't get a depressed dog interested in even trying.

Eventually, they took the dogs by their collars and dragged them through the maze enough times until the dogs began to expect the food, thinking that their good work had produced the food. The dogs were no longer depressed, as was hoped.

When people have no say over their lives, no control, and no ability to do anything to change anything in their lives—that can be very depressing. They can lose the will to live. However, you can help people change their lives by giving them a gentle push, or metaphorically dragging them by the collar through the maze. Sometimes that can help. But it has to be done gently and with respect. Everyone needs to know that they are of value and that they have some effect on their own lives.

Your parents are changing; they are losing some of the things they used to be able to do. But they, like all people, need to be valued; they need to have value. You need to respect what they do at the level they can do it. You also need to value the stage they are at in life and the processes through which they are going.

Learn to value mourning. Not all mourning is depression. Depression is defined as negative feelings that persist for more than two weeks. This also includes at least three of the following: sleeping problems, eating problems, lack of interest in favored activities, motor retardation, and feelings of worthlessness.

Mourning is not pathological; mourning is something that's important to do when you've experienced a loss. A life in general is filled with loss. Generally speaking, through most of our lives we must lose something to gain something. For example, when we turn eighteen we lose the security of being supported by our parents. However, we replace that with the ability to go out on our own. This is generally an improvement—a step up—that helps us get through the loss of parental security.

As we get older we discover that there tend to be fewer things to replace what we've lost. The period of mourning may become a little longer. However, you can help your parents find the ability to replace some of the things that *they* have lost. This is an extreme example, but I remember reading a few years ago about a woman who was 103 years old who had her own blog; she was in fact listed as the oldest blogger in the world. Now at 103 she certainly had lost a lot of things in her life, but she had found something else that she could keep in her life no matter how old she got.

I am not suggesting that you all try to turn your parents into bloggers or even get them interested in the Internet. Some of your parents may do that and some may not. Slowing down is part of aging and it can be mourned. There is a difference between slowing down and being depressed, however. Honor the developmental changes — meaning the slowing down — but don't let them slip into depression.

This is one of the reasons that socialization is so very important. There are many clubs and organizations for senior citizens that your parents can join even if they just go to play cards or sit and watch TV. It's something to keep them going. Now my dad wouldn't do that because he didn't like to be around old people. But many elderly people enjoy making new friends their own age.

However, if your parent is not just slowing down or mourning but appears to be depressed, you might want to have them seen by a professional. Just be careful about someone giving them more medication, unless it's a last resort. Some medications might be able to help them, but you have to watch them carefully. Be careful — there are doctors who are very quick to want to mitigate any sadness with medication.

Value the process of mourning, and help your parents value it also. Talk about it. If they can't, *you* talk about it. For example, one of the things that elderly people can mourn is their mobility. When my dad was seventy-five, he could climb into the beams of my attic on a 110-degree day to fix my chandelier. But when he was ninety he had trouble walking from his bedroom to the living room. Talk about it; if your parents can't talk about it, then you can talk about it for them. That doesn't mean that once a day you point out, "It really stinks that you can't walk anymore. Boy, you must really feel terrible." But you can reminisce with them about things that used to happen. *Wouldn't it be nice if they still could do those things? Yes, but it's great that they can still do x, y, or z.*

Margo Arrowsmith

Acknowledging your parents' value may take some patience. If your mom is trying to do a chore around the house and she is doing the best she can and getting it done, eventually it will have value. Just because you could do it faster, easier, or better doesn't mean that the way she does it doesn't have value; a job done is a job done. If going slow bothers you, don't watch. For example, Dad always wanted to feel useful. He could go out to the kitchen; he couldn't stand and do all the dishes but he could go to the kitchen, sit on his walker, and empty the dishes from the dishwasher onto the countertop. Some days he was able to stand up for a few minutes and put a few from the counter into the cupboard. Then he would sit down for awhile, stand up again, and put a few more in the cupboard. It took a long time, but it was important to him to do it. I would never have dreamed of telling him to stop.

Earlier we talked about you finding out what your parents *want* to do and what they *can* do. It's a good thing to assume that they will always do *something*. Know that if they aren't bedridden, then there is some chore in the house they can do. If emptying the dishwasher takes two hours, it takes two hours. I had two Dalmatians when Dad was there. Some people thought this was terrible because he had to get up several times a day to let them in or out. It may have been self-serving, but I think it was good for him. In fact, when it became difficult for him to get up and down, he might not have done it at all if the dogs hadn't needed him.

I also did a video history with Dad. When he was ninety-one we made videos about what it was like to run a small town newspaper in mid-century Iowa. I had a little flip camera and a YouTube account and told Dad that I wanted him to do some recordings about what it was like back then. He didn't want to do it. He was shy and said he had nothing to say. In the first one I asked him questions so he didn't just have to talk, but eventually — as we did more videos — I stopped asking so many questions; he had so much to say and give to history. I didn't edit any of them; they just flowed. The first one was beautiful. It was about three minutes, and it was very good. I put it on YouTube. Back in those days YouTube required that a video couldn't be any more than three or four minutes. He soon had so much to say that I had to remind him to stop because we couldn't do more. Then I found a young woman who was starting a new brick-and-mortar newspaper with her husband, something unusual in this day and age. I did five interviews with her and Dad talking about the differences between the newspaper business then and now.

Dad was able to tell all his friends from high school—and he had some—that he was on the Internet. I don't know how many of them looked it up but there were quite a few hits. It gave him a sense of pride, and of course it was something of value that he had contributed this project to the world.

Your Value

Caring for your parents is important, of great value, and you are doing a good job. You must know that *you* are important. You must never forget your own value in this. You don't have to do it all yourself in order to be valuable; even running a team has value. Watching a football game with your father while the two of you get your blood flowing jumping up and down has great value. Holding hands with your mother has value. Be patient with yourself in this process.

Good Enough Parent Care

In the 1950s, Freud was becoming pop psychology. Blaming mothers for everything was all the fashion. A lot of women were getting very nervous about this until a guy named DW Winicott came along and said that all any kid needed was *good enough mothering*. Winnecott was a pediatrician and a child analyst from England who noticed how a lot of mothers were so anxious that they were doing things wrong. He thought this unnecessary and wrong, and he developed his theory with evidence to combat that growing idea. Well, I'm here to tell you that all your parent needs is *good enough* parent care; they don't need you to do everything perfectly. They don't need you to never be tired; they don't need you to never say the wrong thing. They just need *good enough.* They need to know you love them, that you're usually there, and that they're going to be okay. That's all they need.

Margo Arrowsmith

I once met a woman who was a doctor. She had had a medical practice, but when it came time for her mother to be home, she stopped her practice to stay home with her mother 24/7 until she died several years later. I certainly was not going to tell her she had done the wrong thing; she did what she felt was right for her and her mother. But this really wasn't necessary, although she insisted that her mother absolutely needed her that amount of time and that nobody else could have ever cared for her mother the way she did. This woman may have needed to do this; it may have been the best thing for her. I am not going to judge this person, but it sounded like overkill to me—not just overkill but not *necessary*, and certainly not something you have to do to be valuable. But some people think, *If I can't do it all, and if I can't do it perfectly, I am no good at this.* I'm here to tell you that all you need to be is good *enough*.

Sacrificing too much can very quickly get you to the point of diminishing returns. If you feel better when your parents start to feel guilty that you're doing too much—that's just not going to be good for either one of you. This is why it's important to value you for who you are. Value what you *can* do, and respect what you *can't* do. Understand that at least you have made it possible for your parent to live and to eventually die with dignity. Love is possible, and in the end that is certainly good enough.

The other part of valuing yourself is respecting your boundaries. Boundaries mean that you know where you start and where the other person ends—or when the other person has gone too far.

As I stated earlier, my mother always had a problem seeing me as a separate person, knowing where I began and where she ended. That caused her and me a lot of pain in our lives because it made communication very difficult.

Knowing boundaries means that people can stand by themselves while working together to perform a huge task. Boundaries are what enable you to stand back far enough to see the other person and know that you love him or her, and you can see that the person loves you, too.

Caretaking can be very hard on boundaries, even if you had good ones before. A caretaker can be overprotective—or the caretaker too needy—and boundaries end up dissolving.

This is why it so important to know and value the rules, to know and value the system you have all set up for yourselves. It's why it's important to make things clear.

It's so much harder when you have family—especially a needy family member—living in your house. If you can remember when your children were babies, they certainly had no boundaries; if they wanted something, you knew about it instantly. But as they started to get older and became a little more independent, it calmed down a bit. It's also different at work. When I'm at work, I know the limits as to what my employer can ask of me. I even know the limits as to what my *clients* can ask me. I know the time frame, what I'm supposed to do, and what I don't have to do—and I value that. My healthiest friends know that we can go out, but that we are not available to each other 24/7. When I'm with my friends, we can watch a TV show or a movie together, but they know sometimes I don't want to be interrupted by them talking.

When you're living with your parents, you have boundaries and they have boundaries. You must establish what time is yours. The days I came home and said "Hi Dad, how are you doing? I'm going upstairs,"—I was making a boundary, and he accepted that. He probably had his own. The nights we watched football games we could just talk and carry on all night long. That was important, but equally important were the nights we didn't talk, or weren't in the same room. Dad and I had good boundaries together, and this is important for making this work.

Your parents get boundaries also. If they are capable, their finances are theirs, not yours to poke around in. If they want you to know what's in there, they will tell you. If you are worried about whether or not somebody else got more than you, that's none of your business.

Margo Arrowsmith

Let your parents know what they need to pay for. As long as that is done, it's none of your business. Having to pay for their own food means they get to decide what they're going to buy. I was notorious—and perhaps terrible—for making suggestions to Dad about what would be healthy, but I would never have dreamed of making him eat anything; that was his choice, his boundary. If they pay for help, they get to choose the help they want. They're entitled to like the person who's working with them.

Use the notes page and let your parents participate and write here too. Don't let them get away with not knowing anything about what their value is.

You Can Keep Your Parents At Home

Margo Arrowsmith

You Can Keep Your Parents At Home

Margo Arrowsmith

You Can Keep Your Parents At Home

Margo Arrowsmith

You Can Keep Your Parents At Home

Margo Arrowsmith

Evaluate what you want because what gets measured, gets produced.

– James A. Belasco

There is nothing more notable in Socrates than that he found time, when he was an old man, to learn music and dancing, and thought it time well spent.

– Michel de Montaigne

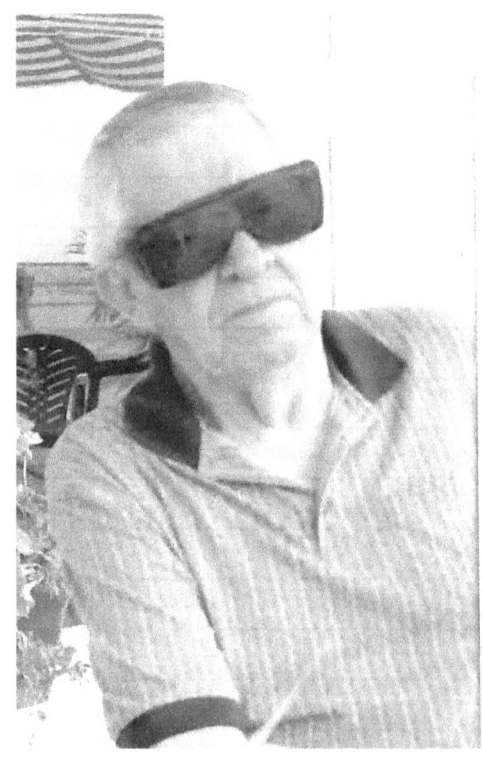

At age 91 Fritz Arrowsmith became a social historian making 15 videos about publishing small town newspapers at midcentury in Iowa. You can see them on Youtube.com under Fritz Arrowsmith

Chapter 9

Evaluate

Every three to four months you need to sit down—preferably with your parents—to go over the plan and keep it in working order.

When Dad was seventy-five he crawled into an attic to do my chandelier. At eighty-five, he had a quintuple bypass but looked like Superman caring for Mom. I just assumed all this would go on forever, but two years later he needed help, and I was caught off guard. Fortunately, the people from Doctors Making House Calls and hospice picked up on what I had missed. I missed it because we really weren't doing evaluations. You need to periodically assess how your parents are doing. It doesn't have to be a long complicated assessment, but you need to do it.

What Is Working

Sit down with your mom or dad, go through the organizational goal list, and check off what's working. You should each make separate lists; you can even ask for input from other team members and then compare the lists. Talk about the differences. They may think they're still doing just fine with walking around the house, but you may have noticed that they've been stumbling. This is the time to say that to them and explore what can be done. Do not assume it's walker time, but look for solutions. You may think you've been fine and dandy with the amount of time you spend with them, but they may think that you've been either spending too little or too much; hopefully they will be able to be honest with you. It's also very important to talk about how the doctors are working out and how the home health aide is working out if they have one. Just go over the whole list.

If something isn't working — or starting not to work — then make a new plan. You can change the plan; for instance, you might say, "Well, you're not doing so well at making your breakfast or lunch anymore, so I think it's time for a home health aide." Or your mom might feel that someone coming in three hours a day is too much; maybe she really only needs the person for two hours. Just make the adjustment and cut back the aide's hours. They might not be big changes—and there might not be any at all — but it's worthwhile to go through that periodically to adjust the plan. Doing this may seem like a bit of a chore, but it's going to keep you happier, it will keep your parent home longer, and it's going to keep everybody healthier *and* save money.

What Is Not Working

The process is pretty much the same, but this time you're going to talk about what *isn't* working; make the lists and compare. Focus on physical issues and mental issues. If your parents are not doing as much activity find out why. It's possible that they are not doing as much mentally or socially because they're more tired, had a fight with a friend, or got more involved with the Internet. Don't assume the worst. Your parents are allowed to wind down after all.

If they are depressed, suggest they talk to someone. Dad stopped watching his beloved basketball. He had been a basketball player and fan his entire life. He and Mom were crazy basketball people but suddenly he wouldn't watch it anymore. He still watched football, but rather than just assume he was depressed I asked him why. It turned out that because of his macular degeneration it was harder for him to see, even with his flat screen TV. It was harder for him to see the basketball. For some reason, it was easier for him to watch football, perhaps because there wasn't as much constant action. But it wasn't depression, although there was a loss.

If one of their complaints is that you're going out too much, talk about it. You are still going to go out, by the way, but find out if there is something they need from you while you are there. You could suggest that maybe one night a week the two of you go out for dinner together, while you go out with others on other nights. Frankly, they probably don't want you to give up everything—even though that may have been one of your worst fantasies.

You now know to ask the team to help identify any problems. Remember, though, that each of them only has a small—but important—part of the picture. You and your parents see the whole picture. If the problem has been identified, they may have some solutions for how to fix it. Balance it out by listening to all of them. What one may see as depression someone else may recognize as Dad not moving around as much because of problems walking. You also might want to check to see what time of day different things are being noticed. If only one person is noticing something, it could just be that there is something about the morning or about two o'clock in the afternoon. If everyone agrees there is a problem, what should you do about it? Getting a wheelchair or a new bathroom configuration might be the solution.

Just remember not to panic. A problem doesn't mean that suddenly nothing is working; it just means that the plan might need some tweaking.

Changing Needs

Don't confuse your needs with your parents' needs, and don't confuse your frustrations with theirs.

It broke my heart when Dad stopped watching basketball, but while he may have missed it, it didn't really seem to bother him that much. You may want your parent to stay exactly the same, but that may not be a need of theirs. Winding down is part of aging, and people do it at different speeds and in different ways. Don't try to force them to hang on to everything. I was so surprised when Dad didn't want to watch basketball anymore, but he was changing. That was my issue to deal with.

There is a song called "Old Man River" from the Broadway play, *Showboat*. It's sung in a deep poignant baritone, and the line that always kills me is, *I'm tired of livin' and scared of dyin'.*" Dad was never tired of living, and he was not afraid of dying.

Dad never got over being interested in politics; as a lifelong Republican he wasn't a fan of Barack Obama, but he was very interested in seeing how Obamacare would turn out. So while he lost interest in basketball—because of his eyes, not because of depression—he still maintained other interests and gained some new ones. The basketball bothered me more than it bothered him. When I evaluated, it turned out that it was more of *my* issue than Dad's, and it was something to be left alone.

So again, understand that your purpose is to keep your parents with happiness and dignity as long as they are alive. You may have added other purposes—and that's fine—but that is the basics.

Evaluate Your Own Aging

Mom tried to keep her parents at an apartment in town, and then she tried to keep them with us. She worked more than full time, and there just wasn't any help available at the time—or none that she would use. She finally had to put them in a nursing home, and she never got over it.

I'll never forget the first time I went to visit the home; it was an old broken down house with a bunch of old men sitting around staring into space in Grandpa's room while Grandma laid in bed in another room. I was seventeen and I loved my grandparents; my heart was broken, just as Mom's was. I was also horrified that this may have been my future. I made the first of many vows to never end up like that.

While taking care of Dad, I was no longer a teen and so narcissistic, but I still worried about what I would be like at ninety-two and what I could do to make it different for me. Taking care of your aging parents may be a wake-up call to start living *your* aging with intention and not with fear, but with a plan to be amazing while you're doing it.

I did an article for an online organization about elder people who had done amazing things. There was the previously mentioned 103-year-old woman who was blogging. People in their nineties were skydiving and scuba diving, and a woman had gotten her college degree at ninety-five—all sorts of wonderful things. After thirty-four years of trying, Diana Nyad finally became the first person to swim from Cuba to the Florida Keys without a shark tank around her. Valerie Harper was on *Dancing With the Stars* at seventy-four, with a brain tumor no less.

I have pictures in my home of my grandparents on their fiftieth wedding anniversary and pictures of my mom and dad on *their* fiftieth wedding anniversary. Grandma and Grandpa were about four or five years older than Mom and Dad, but they looked twenty years older, if not more. Mom and Dad had not done much taking care of themselves, but they lived at a time when life was different. They had expectations of aging with a different attitude than Grandma and Grandpa had, and it showed.

Aging is not for sissies is something I believe Katharine Hepburn first said, and it's true—but it's also not for those who give up. I have cautioned you to not get on your mom and dad for how they choose to do their aging; clearly it's their business. Make suggestions and try to help them do it better, but know that they're going to do what they want to do. However, as you care for your parents it's also time to start to make some decisions about how *you* want do it.

It's a good thing to balance between doing it to the hilt and being graceful about it all. Grandpa was very angry on his deathbed, cursing and very upset. My dad was very graceful. Of course he didn't know he was dying, but he knew he was close. Grandpa was in his seventies. He was very young to be so sick, so maybe he had a good reason to be angry. But the issue is balancing between living your life to the hilt, staying active and young as long as you can, but also aging and letting go gracefully.

Taking care of your parents is a time to start doing some heavy duty evaluating of your own life. Of course, if you're not at that point yet, you don't have to wait that long, but caretaking is a time when you have to face the future.

Health

When I went to see Grandma and Grandpa in their nursing home when I was seventeen, I was horrified—not just that they were there but that someday I might be there too.

It's time now to start evaluating how active you are, even if you have to spend a lot more time at home with your parents. You could always get a tread climber, treadmill, or bicycle. If you're feeling tied to the house, that's no reason not to be active. There are all sorts of videos you can play. I once had a great yoga video that really helped me get into yoga. While they warn you against starting and stopping and starting again, doing it sometimes is better than not doing it at all. Supposedly, every time you stop and then start again later, you are essentially starting from scratch. However, in my experience, that is not true. When I got my tread climber it took me a long time to work up to being able to do it for an hour. However, I can now stop for a month or two, and it just takes me a couple of days to work up to being able to work out for an hour. I am not suggesting you do this, but I have gone a year without doing any exercise and when I started again I knew I could do things I could not do when I was thirty—which was when I first started doing major exercise. So while I do not suggest the stopping and starting—and I'm working very hard to get myself out of that—it's better than not getting any exercise at all.

Now is the time to do what you have to do to stay as well as possible for as long as you can.

You have to be healthy, but what else do you want to do? Start doing an evaluation of yourself. What is your life going to look like at age seventy? Eighty? Ninety? Look at the list of old people—and yes, ninety can be called old—and the things they do. Perhaps there is something there for you. The popular movie, *The Bucket List*, shows things to do before you die. Make a bucket list and keep adding to it. The activities don't all have to be travel or daredevil; they could be things like learning a language or painting. They don't have to be super active experiences; remember the ninety-five-year-old college graduate and the blogger? They also don't have to cost you a lot of money or require a huge nest egg. It would be nice to be able to travel the world and hike through Australia, but you can also go hike through the local park.

What's important is that you start to evaluate what you want your aging to be like and to figure out how to do it.

Use the note pages to begin the evaluation process exercises. You may want the evaluation of your own aging to be private, then use separate pages for that, but put the evaluation of your plan here for all to see.

Margo Arrowsmith

You Can Keep Your Parents At Home

Margo Arrowsmith

You Can Keep Your Parents At Home

Margo Arrowsmith

You Can Keep Your Parents At Home

Margo Arrowsmith

You Can Keep Your Parents At Home

Margo Arrowsmith

You Can Keep Your Parents At Home

Margo Arrowsmith

"Go back?" he thought. "No good at all! Go sideways? Impossible! Go forward? Only thing to do! On we go!" So up he got, and trotted along with his little sword held in front of him and one hand feeling the wall, and his heart all of a patter and a pitter.

–J.R.R. Tolkien, *The Hobbit*

Fritz Arrowsmith and his great grand son, Nico. Life moves on.

Chapter 10

Moving Forward

The L.O.V.E. formula is a basic strategy to follow to keep your mom or dad at home while you keep your job, your life, and your sanity. Remember that this is something that you will do with your parents as much as possible. Share this with them if you feel they are up to it. Have them read the book or parts of it. They may only be interested in the part about organizing a team, but get them as involved as they can be; this is about them.

However, if they are fine with going through the exercises in this book–although I know that's not very likely with people of their generation–let them do them but don't push them.

They can talk about letting go of what they could do, their houses, and lots of things. It can be done in a way that celebrates their lives · and also looks to the future. Do a project such as the history project I did with my dad.

Organizing is something they can definitely participate in. They should participate in the medical summary if at all possible, but they can also participate in the rest of it. They know if they think it would be fun to have somebody come and play cards. They know if they want to go to the local senior citizen center to play cards instead. They know what they want to do.

Your parents need to participate in the interviewing of prospective team members. They may not be very active, but you need to get their input as to what they think. Remind them the money spent here will last a lot longer than it will last in an assisted living or nursing home; so ultimately this is very thrifty.

A history project could help them continue to *value* themselves even if there is nothing left that they can do.

Make them part of periodic evaluations. Find out what they are happy about, find out what they would like to be different, and then see if it's possible to do any of those things. Make sure they understand your limits. The clearer you are about your boundaries, the more likely they are to be honored.

And *evaluate* to know where you stand.

Take care of yourself while you take care of them. There are things that you can do now for both of you: stay healthy, stay active, stay interested, and find a friend you can talk to who will listen and let you solve your problems.

Find a group of people who are doing the same things. I found that many organized groups never meet, but if you organize one yourself you can make sure it meets. Perhaps all those groups need is just somebody to take the reins.

Don't forget to find a professional for yourself if necessary.

And above all, love your parents and be with them while planning for an amazing aging of your own.

Dear Reader,

Thank you for participating in this journey. I trust as you read my story that you gained information that will be helpful to you in your experiences with your parents and your aging.

For us to be truly helpful to each other, this must be an interactive process. This first edition will be expanded as I hear from more people who have successes and bumps in taking care or thinking about taking care of their parents while improving their own aging.

Go to www.YourBestParentCareTips.com

Follow us on Facebook at KeepYourParentsHome

Yours Truly,

Margo Arrowsmith, LCSW

Resources

This list includes just some of the many resources that are there for you.

Go to www.bestparentcaretips.com to find updated lists.

If you have any information about any organization here or new sources, please feel free to let us know, and we will add your information.

AARP
http://www.aarp.org/

AARP Grandparent Information Center
http://assets.aarp.org/www.aarp.org_/articles/families/gp_visitation_faq.pdf

Administration on Aging
http://www.aoa.gov/

Adult Children of Aging Parents
http://adultchildrenofagingparents.com/

Margo Arrowsmith

American Association of Homes and Services for the Aging
http://www.organizedwisdom.com/American-Association-of-Homes-and-Services-for-the-Aging/wt/med

American Health Assistance Foundation
http://www.charitywatch.org/articles/Americanhealthassistance.html

Americans for Better Care of the Dying
http://www.caringcommunity.org/helpful-resources/models-research/americans-for-better-care-of-the-dying/

Brookdale Center on Aging
http://brookdale.org/

Catholic Charities
http://catholiccharitiesusa.org/

Consumer Coalition for Quality Health Care
http://www.lead411.com/company_ConsumerCoalitionforQualityHealthCare_1189907.html

Corporation for National Service
http://www.nationalservice.gov/

Department of Veterans Affairs
http://www.va.gov/

Elder Care Locator
  http://www.eldercare.gov/Eldercare.NET/Public/Index.aspx

Funeral and Memorial Societies of America
  http://onlinecaskets.net/faq/consumer-rights/famsa.html

National Cremation Society
  http://www.nationalcremation.com/

Generations United
  http://gu.org/

Grey Panthers
  http://gu.org/

Growth House
  http://www.growthhouse.org/

Hospice Foundation of America
  http://www.hospicefoundation.org/

Leadership Counsel of Aging Organizations
  http://www.aarp.org/livable-communities/learn/demographics/info-12-2012/leadership-council-aging-orgs-website.html

Margo Arrowsmith

Little Brothers' Friends of the Elderly
http://www.littlebrothers.org/

Medicare Rights Center
http://www.medicarerights.org/

National Academy of Elder Law Attorneys
http://elder-law.laws.com/elder-law-attorneys/national-academy-of-elder-law-attorneys

National Caregivers Library
www.caregiverslibrary.org/

National Adult Day Care Services
http://nadsa.org/

National Institute on Aging
http://nadsa.org/

National Association of Professional Geriatric Case Managers
http://www.caremanager.org/

National Citizens' Coalition for Nursing Home Reform
http://www.geronurseonline.org

National Committee To Preserve Social Security and Medicare
http://www.ncpssm.org/

National Institute of Senior Centers
http://www.ncoa.org/national-institute-of-senior-centers/

National Center on Elder Abuse
http://www.ncea.aoa.gov/

Older Women's League
http://owl-national.org/

Social Security Administration
http://www.ssa.gov/

House of Representatives: Find and contact your representative
http://www.house.gov/representatives/find/

United States Senate: Find and contact your senator
http://www.senate.gov/general/contact_information/senators_cfm.cfm

Well Spouse Association
http://wellspouse.org/

www.ingramcontent.com/pod-product-compliance
Lightning Source LLC
Chambersburg PA
CBHW062012180426
43199CB00034B/2489